The Black Archive #19

The Eleventh Hour

By Jon Arnold

Published May 2018 by Obverse Books

Cover Design © Cody Schell

Text © Jon Arnold, 2018

Range Editors: James Cooray Smith, Philip Purser-Hallard

Jon would like to thank:

Paul, for the idea
Phil, Jim and Stu for having me back
Carolyn and Eddie for letting me disappear
Stephen and Heather, for prompting the family discussion
The Twilight Shift for sanity and good times
James, for the patience

Also Available

For Eddie, the Impossible Boy Adventurer

'...every revolution is a palace revolution. Nobody can be first: all you can be is the latest.'

[Clive James][1]

---

[1] James, Clive, *Play All: A Bingewatcher's Notebook*, p176.

CONTENTS

OVERVIEW

Serial Title: *The Eleventh Hour*

Writer: Steven Moffat

Director: Adam Smith

Original UK Transmission Dates: 3 April 2010

Running Time: 1hr 4m 54s

UK Viewing Figures: 10.0 million

Regular Cast: Matt Smith (The Doctor), Karen Gillan (Amy Pond)

Recurring Cast: Arthur Darvill (Rory Williams), Caitlin Blackwood (Amelia)

Guest Cast: Nina Wadia (Dr Ramsden), Marcello Magni (Barney Collins), Perry Benson (Ice cream man), Annette Crosbie (Mrs Angelo), Tom Hopper (Jeff), Arthur Cox (Mr Henderson), Olivia Coleman (Mother), Eden Monteath (Child 1), Merin Monteath (Child 2), David de Keyser (Atraxi voice), William Wilde (Prisoner Zero voice), Patrick Moore (Himself)

Antagonists: Prisoner Zero, The Atraxi.

Sequels: To some extent, all the 11th Doctor's TV era, but particularly *The Time of Angels / Flesh and Stone*, *Vampires of Venice*, *The Pandorica Opens / The Big Bang* (TV, 2010), *The God Complex* (TV, 2011) and *The Time of the Doctor* (TV, 2013) .

Responses:

'*The Eleventh Hour* [...] feels like an absolute triumph. A whole new world of regulars is seamlessly introduced, the story has both pace and complexity, and it's refreshing not be in London again. The Atraxi eyeball-ship has to be one of the most beautiful design creations the **Doctor Who** teams have ever come up with'

[Daniel Martin, *The Guardian*]

'[I]t felt a bit routine, as if keeping the machine running was now the paradigm. There was none of the over-the-top exuberance, in either comic or melodramatic terms, of the Davies years; one attempt at that, an early sequence in which the Doctor spits out a series of meals while trying to determine what food he now likes, was grimly unfunny.'

[Mike Hale, *The New York Times*]

SYNOPSIS

One night a young orphan girl named **Amelia Pond** is praying to Santa for assistance when a blue box crashes to Earth in her back garden and a raggedy man comes out. He is hungry, but rejects almost all the food Amelia can supply. Amelia, whose aunt is away, eventually asks the man, the **Doctor**, to help her with a scary crack in the wall of her bedroom.

The Doctor quickly discovers that the crack is not in the wall, but in the fabric of reality. He opens it, and a giant eyeball peers through, informing them that 'Prisoner Zero has escaped'. The Doctor closes the crack but is distracted by his damaged box, the TARDIS. Realising he must move it into the future to stabilise the engines, he promises Amelia he will come back for her in five minutes. She packs a small suitcase and waits for him.

The TARDIS returns in daylight, and the Doctor has realised he was missing a vital point about Amy's house. He goes inside, but is knocked out and handcuffed by a policewoman. She tells him Amelia is gone, and that she lives here now. He tries to explain that **Prisoner Zero** escaped through the crack into a room in the house, which it has been hiding from the occupants. The policewoman insists on entering the now-revealed room, and sees the alien Zero. She and the Doctor flee the house pursued by Zero, now in the form of a man with a dog. The policewoman reveals that she is Amelia, now known as **Amy**. The Doctor has been gone 12 years, much of which she has spent in therapy dealing with her abandonment issues. She is wearing the police uniform she uses for kissogram work.

The **Atraxi**, a space police force hunting Prisoner Zero, broadcast a demand that humanity surrender the escapee or they will destroy the Earth. They cause a solar eclipse as a show of strength. The Doctor frantically searches Amy's village, Leadworth, for Prisoner Zero. He meets Amy's boyfriend **Rory**, her friend **Jeff** and his grandmother **Mrs Angelo**, who all remember him from Amy's childhood stories and games about her 'Raggedy Doctor'. Rory, a nurse, recognises the dog-walking man as a coma patient at the local hospital, and the Doctor realises that Zero is forming telepathic links with unconscious people to take their shapes. Amy and Rory go to the hospital, where they find Prisoner Zero in the form of a mother with two small girls. Meanwhile the Doctor uses Jeff's laptop to gatecrash an online meeting of experts discussing the crisis, including TV astronomer **Patrick Moore**, and asks them to spread a computer virus which will reset all the world's clocks to zero.

The Doctor joins Amy and Rory. The virus has attracted the Atraxi, still appearing as a giant eyeball, to Leadworth, and he has texted them photos of all the prisoner's avatars. Zero disguises itself by knocking Amy out and taking her form instead – more specifically, that of little Amelia. The Doctor reminds the unconscious Amy of her meeting with Zero, and the alien ends up impersonating its own real shape. Before it is arrested by the Atraxi it cryptically predicts to the Doctor that 'The Pandorica will open' and 'Silence will fall.'

The Doctor summons back the departing Atraxi and scolds them for threatening the Earth, telling them that he is the planet's protector. He leaves for a 'quick hop' in the newly repaired TARDIS, accidentally returning two years later than he intended. This time though, he takes Amy with him, promising to have her home by the next day. Among the possessions she leaves behind are drawings and dolls of the 'Raggedy Doctor', and a wedding dress waiting to be worn.

PREHISTORY: 'SOME NEW MAN GOES SAUNTERING AWAY'

For all the nerves beforehand[2], the revival of **Doctor Who** in 2005 can in retrospect be seen as a low-risk, high-reward gamble by the BBC. A flagship Saturday night drama failing may have been a temporary embarrassment, but would almost certainly have become a footnote in otherwise successful careers: a question for interviewers to ask Russell T Davies, Christopher Eccleston and Billie Piper. In terms of the show itself, the worst that might have happened can be gleaned from the reaction to *Doctor Who* (1996), which was, in UK transmission terms at least, essentially a failed pilot for a proposed series. A small new generation of fans would have been created and they and the existing fandom would almost certainly have continued as they had done since the BBC had ended production of the show in 1989. As it stood before the 2005 series, **Doctor Who** was essentially a moribund property: the worst that could happen would be that the show would fall back into an existence centred around the BBC novels, Big Finish audios and *Doctor Who Magazine* (DWM).

All that changed dramatically with the broadcast of *Rose* (2005), when it became clear that Davies's version of **Doctor Who** was a precision-engineered weapon of mass entertainment perfectly tailored to Saturday night television. It blended the cheap thrills of pulp science-fiction with the character-driven drama of soap opera and added a dash of structure from reality television to produce one

---

[2] 'I'm amazed that we worried, that we were scared the show would die a death.' Davies, Russell T, and Benjamin Cook, *Doctor Who: The Writer's Tale, The Final Chapter,* pp681-82.

of the great British dramatic successes of the early 21st century[3]. As Davies asked when rewatching it in 2009: 'how could you not watch **Doctor Who** when it's that good?!'[4] The episode delivered 10.81 million viewers, the seventh most watched programme of the week and was the highest placed episode since 1975[5]. It was, in time, established that it was the most watched drama transmitted on British television that year[6].

The BBC announced a second series and the ultimate accolade of a Christmas episode four days after the episode was aired[7]. In 45 minutes the show went from a loved but often mocked nostalgia piece to one of the BBC's flagship dramas. It would go on to better these achievements: the 2007 Christmas episode *Voyage of the Damned* would be the second most watched programme not only of the week but of the entire year and, after a near miss by *The Stolen Earth* (2008), the final episode of Davies's last full season, *Journey's End* (2008), became the only **Doctor Who** episode up to that point to top the UK ratings for the week[8].

This was achieved while the show proved it was not dependent on particular cast members to survive: Eccleston had been replaced by David Tennant after the first season and Piper had departed at the end of the second season with the show remaining successful.

---

[3] For an in-depth discussion of this see Arnold, Jon, *The Black Archive #1: Rose*, Chapter 4.

[4] Davies and Cook, *The Writer's Tale*, p682.

[5] When episode 2 of *The Ark in Space* was the fifth most watched programme of the week.

[6] 'TV Since 1981'.

[7] 'New Doctor Who series confirmed'.

[8] Referring only to its broadcast on BBC One as per official BARB figures.

Indeed, none of the seasons overseen by Davies, including the specials which ended his run, retained the same regular cast from the previous year. This concealed that, behind the different chemistry brought by the combination of lead actors, the storytelling engine of the show itself essentially remained unchanged until 2009:

> 'This show has drawn more and more people to it as time has gone on, and it hasn't increased its audience by changing; it's done so by staying the same, by being consistent, by never flinching.'[9]

Whilst individual episodes may have stretched the format of the show established in *Rose*[10], the story which underpinned each season remained unchanged: each series is essentially the story of the relationship between the Doctor and his companion, set against the backdrop of a plot which is hinted at throughout the season until it is exposed and dealt with in a suitably dramatic fashion in a multi-episode season finale. **Doctor Who** is often cited as having a 'flexible format'[11], an ability to adapt itself to survive and avoid going stale. The Davies era became an exercise in mining a formula as far as it could be taken: the season ending stakes became ever bigger to conceal this. The comforting repetition with slight variations allowed the show to survive alongside the other long-running Saturday night successes Davies drew on when bringing the show back: the mainstays of British Saturday night television schedules in the 21st

---

[9] Davies and Cook, *The Writer's Tale*, p685.
[10] Often by Davies himself, with the likes of *Love & Monsters* (2006) and *Gridlock* (2007).
[11] See, for example, Howe, David J, Mark Stammers and Stephen James Walker, *Doctor Who: The Television Companion,* p157; or Burk, Graeme and Robert Smith?, *Who Is the Doctor*, p153.

century have all followed rigid, popular formats to long-running ratings success[12]. In this respect Davies can perhaps be seen as a dramatic equivalent of **The X Factor** svengali Simon Cowell: the man behind the curtain happy to publicise the series and, to a degree, pull back that metaphorical drapery and show the inner workings of the industry.

Whilst the series had easily weathered the departure of its onscreen stars it had not proven that it could survive the departure of its creative engine and the accompanying likely changes to its format.

Davies officially turned down a fifth series of **Doctor Who** on 11 April 2007[13]. This had been his plan since *Doomsday* (2006) was filmed (between November 2005 and January 2006):

> 'We decided that we'd have a fourth series (David's third), with a big ending, after which we'd take the show off the air, just for a short while, apart from the odd Special, so that we could have a breather, and a new production team could settle in, find its feet, and prepare for Series Five. [...] Julie, Phil, Jane and I committed to that initial promise, and we're sticking to our word. That promise means that the fifth series

---

[12] Saturday nights have been dominated by variations on the talent contest formula such as **Strictly Come Dancing** (2004-), **The X Factor** (2004-) and **The Voice** (2012-). These can themselves be seen as variations on the old themes; the likes of **New Faces** (1973-77, 1986-88), **Opportunity Knocks** (1956-77, 1987-90) and **Thank Your Lucky Stars** (1961-66). It's an example of the history of television largely being evolution of basic formats.

[13] Davies and Cook, *The Writer's Tale*, p83.

option does not exist for me. [...] It's flattering and all that but it ain't gonna happen.'[14]

On 17 July Davies emailed Steven Moffat to gauge his interest in succeeding him[15]. Moffat confirmed to Davies on 28 September that he would take up the post, though this would not be finalised until 26 October. He was the obvious choice to succeed Davies: he had created and written the entirety of four different series for the BBC[16], as well as writing every episode of the Children's ITV series **Press Gang** (1989-93). The three **Doctor Who** stories of his which aired prior to his appointment were critically acclaimed: Moffat won the 2008 Best Writer BAFTA award for *Blink* (2007) and each of his stories appeared in the top 11 of DWM's 2009 *Mighty 200* poll[17]. No other writer could match the combination of success, acclaim and long-term love for the show[18]. As he said on the announcement of

[14] Davies and Cook, *The Writer's Tale*, p84.

[15] Davies and Cook, *The Writer's Tale*, p161. Davies explicitly points out on the following page that he was not choosing his successor.

[16] **Joking Apart** (1991-95), **Chalk** (1997), **Coupling** (2000-2004) and **Jekyll** (2007).

[17] *Silence in the Library / Forest of the Dead* (2008), broadcast after his appointment was announced, appeared at 24. *The Empty Child / The Doctor Dances* (2005) and *Blink* remained in the top ten of DWM's 50th anniversary poll, with the only more popular 21st-century episode being Moffat's own *The Day of the Doctor* (2013).

[18] Of the other writers with experience on the series to that point, only Chris Chibnall and Matthew Graham offered a similar profile in terms of experience. Chibnall had developed and been head writer on **Born and Bred** (2002-05) and had been showrunner for the first two seasons of **Torchwood** (2006-11), while Graham had co-created **Life on Mars** (2006-07). Even if interested, both writers were busy on other projects, Chibnall on **Law and Order UK** (2009-14) and **Camelot** (2011) and Graham on **Ashes to Ashes** (2008-10)., the

his taking over, his career was 'a secret plan to get the job.'[19]

Moffat would also have to make the biggest decision any new showrunner would have had to make early on: to work out who his leading man would be. He initially asked David Tennant to continue for one more season in the role, outlining his plans if the actor wished to continue. After considering, Tennant decided to decline the offer and move on, as per his pact with Davies.

Moffat essentially inherited a series in better shape than it ever had been. Davies departed with the two-part story *The End of Time* (2009-10): a decadent festival of excess which was the **Doctor Who** equivalent of imperial follies such as *Cleopatra* (1963) or *Caligula* (1979). It saw the departures of the Doctor, showrunner and several key creative personnel, and its second episode was the second most watched show of the first week of 2010[20]. **Doctor Who** would return

---

sequel to **Life on Mars.** Both had written only a single **Doctor Who** episode to this point, and neither were as generally well received as Moffat's.

[19] It's important to note here that Moffat's interviews generally feature weapons-grade self-deprecation and as many jokes as any of his **Doctor Who** episodes. This may be why he expressed a distaste for print interviews in his second appearance on **Toby Hadoke's Who's Round** podcast – verbal jokes can often be misconstrued or fall flat on the page when stripped of context and performance.

[20] Official BARB figures gave a rating of 11.79 million for the episode's broadcast on BBC One, behind the New Year's Day episode of **EastEnders** (1985-). Adding in the figures for the simulcast on the BBC's HD channel, as would be adopted as industry standard within months, gives a total of 12.27 million viewers, which would make it the most watched show of that week. It was again the most watched drama of the entire year.

just three months later with a new Doctor, a new companion and its new head writer. Could Moffat replicate Davies's success? Could the relatively unknown Matt Smith effectively replace one of the most popular actors ever to play the role? In short, was the outrageous success of **Doctor Who**'s latest golden era essentially the product of Tennant and Davies's chemistry? Could different personnel maintain the show's level of success?

Doctor Who needed to prove itself all over again.

CHAPTER 1: 'NEW MOUTH, NEW RULES'

Television is, by nature, a medium of compromises. The collaborative nature of production means it is nearly impossible for a show to reach the screen as originally intended – for instance, a director's choice of shot or actor's line reading may entirely alter the intent of a scene. The Doctor who arrived on screen in the final minutes of episode 2 of *The End of Time* is a case in point. Nothing about the incarnation portrayed by Matt Smith conformed to Steven Moffat's original vision for the part.

As already mentioned, Moffat's first idea was to ask David Tennant to return for one last series. This was a commercially and artistically shrewd decision – Tennant staying on would have largely concealed the sweeping changes in the production office, and he was clearly still popular with the public. The plot arc of the series would have been similarly structured to the one eventually seen on screen, though the emphasis of the character arc would have changed: it would have played out the end of one incarnation rather than the beginning of a new one. Instead of a new Doctor landing in Leadworth, the Doctor who met Amelia would have been the 10th Doctor at a point immediately prior to his regeneration[21]. An earlier version of Tennant's Doctor would then have met the adult Amy and travelled with her, before coming full circle by regenerating in the

---

[21] Moffat would use this concept of regeneration as an audience teaser in his final episodes: the pre-credits sequence for *World Enough and Time* (2017) featured a regenerating 12th Doctor but the regeneration would not happen until the final moments of *Twice Upon a Time* (2017), a full three episodes (and several months) later. Never waste a good idea. (Moffat, Steven, 'Ask Steven Moffat', DWM #459, p6.)

last episode of the season. This scenario was ruled out almost immediately by Tennant confirming his decision to leave[22].

With Tennant ruled out, Moffat's ideal for the next Doctor was tempered by the practicalities of television production:

> 'The show is really tough for a super-fit David Tennant so you might kill someone who takes on the role in their 60s[23] [...] I think the Doctor will always be about 40.'[24]

Although public statements around the time suggested that Matt Smith was always the first choice for the past, this appears not to have been the case. In DWM #500, speaking about Pearl Mackie's casting as Bill Potts, Moffat was asked if the next Doctor could be non-white:

> 'I certainly don't think there's a problem with making the Doctor black, which is why it should happen one day. I mean,

---

[22] Tennant's decision to leave seems to have inadvertently started a trend – each of the executive producers generally referred to as showrunner has cast a new Doctor upon taking over. This is in stark contrast to the 20th-century BBC run of the show, where all the Doctors following Hartnell were cast by an incumbent production team, many of whom then almost immediately left the series.

[23] Moffat would go on to cast the 73-year-old John Hurt and 55-year-old Peter Capaldi, the oldest and third oldest actors to play a unique incarnation of the Doctor at the time of their first appearance, and 75-year-old David Bradley in the reprised role of William Hartnell's first Doctor. Bradley is the second oldest actor ever to play the part, after Tom Baker, who was 83 at the time of his cameo in *The Day of the Doctor*.

[24] Moffat, Steven, quoted in Pixley, Andrew, 'Just Like Starting Over', *The Doctor Who Companion: Series 5 Volume 1*, p9.

we've tried. The part has been offered to a black actor. But for various reasons, it didn't work out.'[25]

Given that the casting of Tennant and Capaldi were essentially faits accomplis and the only known alternative offer made before the casting of Christopher Eccleston was a speculative offer to Hugh Grant, the only point to which Moffat could be referring would be the casting sessions for the 11th Doctor. In 2016, citing an unnamed source who worked on the show at the time, the *Radio Times* website named Chiwetel Ejiofor as the actor who had turned the part down, due to being 'unable to agree terms with the Corporation.'[26] Ejiofor would have been in the age range Moffat was looking for[27] and, at the same time, provide the kind of shake-up to the show's formula that Moffat has proven to be keen on.

Instead Moffat shook up the show in a way unexpected even to himself: he and his fellow producers would cast the youngest actor ever to play the show's lead role and, against his own generally contrarian instincts, it would be an actor in a relatively similar phase of his career to Tennant. Tennant's casting as the Doctor came after leading roles in two highly regarded BBC One shows in quick succession[28]. Matt Smith's career was in a similar place, with the role

---

[25] Quoted in Cook, Benjamin, 'This Is It. I'm Going to Push the Button. When I Do There's No Going Back. I'm About to End What Will Be the Best Job I Ever Have', DWM #500, p61.

[26] Dowell, Ben, 'Was Chiwetel Ejiofor the black actor offered the role of the 11th Doctor ahead of Matt Smith?'

[27] 'I thought it's mid-30s to mid-40s... young enough to run but old enough to look like they can be King of the Universe' (Moffat, Steven, quoted in Spilsbury, Tom, 'The Time Is Now!', DWM #418, p18).

[28] **Blackpool** (2004) (transmitted as **Viva Blackpool** in the US) and **Casanova** (2005). **Casanova** was first broadcast on BBC Three but

of Jim Taylor in BBC One adaptations of two of Philip Pullman's four **Sally Lockhart** novels[29], and in two BBC Two dramas: as one of the four leads in **Party Animals** (2007) and in a secondary role in the police drama **Moses Jones** (2009). Of these roles, none are particularly indicative of how he would eventually play the Doctor in the way that Tennant's role in **Casanova** (2005) would point to his eventual performance[30]. Indeed, prior to the broadcast of *The Eleventh Hour* (2010) Moffat made a point of how he felt the role of the Doctor was a more natural fit for Smith than his role in **Moses Jones** or Dr Watson in **Sherlock** (2010-) (a part he auditioned for before it was given to Martin Freeman), and that his previous work had little bearing on how Smith would play the role:

> '...as much as he was a struggling, but brilliantly at accomplishing, Dr Watson, he just utterly got the Doctor [...] He so **got** it in every move. He was like Matt Smith unleashed! It was like he could just act in the way he always **wanted** to, as opposed to the way he always **tried** to. He's brilliant in

---

was repeated on the main BBC channel within three weeks of its first airing.

[29] These were broadcast under the umbrella title **The Sally Lockhart Mysteries** (2006-2007) and also starred Billie Piper. Smith would work with Piper again on an episode of **The Secret Diary of a Call Girl** (2007-2011).

[30] The value of **Casanova** as an indicator of Tennant's performance perhaps lies in it also being a leading role written by Russell T Davies and the first indication of how Tennant would interpret Davies's scripts. None of the shows Smith had starred in are particularly close to Steven Moffat's style of writing.

Moses Jones, but he's trying to play a geezer. Matt's **so not** a geezer...'[31]

Rather than a dramatic statement of intent, this decision echoed the history of the series from the early 1980s, when Tom Baker was replaced by the previous youngest actor to play the part, Peter Davison. This may not be unintentional, if possibly subconscious, on Moffat's part. Although he has been critical of other eras of the show, Moffat has been consistent in his praise of the Davison era, saying as far back as 1995 that 'it still stands up', that it's 'well constructed' and that Davison himself was 'extremely good as the Doctor'[32]. Whilst other producers may have baulked at casting a young man as the Doctor, it's likely that Moffat's recall of Davison's successful performance in the role meant that he was receptive to the idea of a younger Doctor[33].

Davison's approach may also have been a template for Moffat when it came to writing for a younger Doctor. The approach suggested by the production crew can be summed up as 'old man trapped in a

---

[31] Spilsbury, 'The Time is Now!', p18.

[32] Quoted in Bishop, David, 'Four Writers, One Discussion'.

[33] This would not be the only parallel to Davison's casting: both actors recorded their first stories out of sequence, ostensibly to allow themselves to settle into the role and find their performance before recording an opening story which would see them disoriented. Davison disputes this in his autobiography, claiming that the reason the recording took place out of sequence 'was the minor inconvenience that there was no script' for *Castrovalva* (1982) (Davison, Peter, *Is There Life Outside the Box?*, p170).

young body'[34] and Moffat's initial interviews about Smith's casting encouraged parallels:

> 'Matt is an extraordinary fellow... he's like a young man built by old men from memory.'[35]

> 'Matt is a hot young bloke – a very, very handsome young man – who is nonetheless just genetically a little bit like Magnus Pyke, or whoever the modern equivalent would be.'[36]

The comparison to Pyke (1908-92), the go-to eccentric scientist for British television from the 1960s until the late 1980s, is not simply Moffat dealing in idle shorthand. Track down a clip of Pyke and you can see parallels in to Smith's penchant for odd, startling movements and fondness for emphasising his lines with physical gestures as much as vocal inflections: it's something that can be seen in his interview for the **Doctor Who Confidential** episode which announced his casting, and as late as *The Time of the Doctor* (2013) with the way he rolls his hands when delivering the line 'You gotta keep moving'[37].

Not only is this drawing on elements of Smith's own personality, but it's also where you can see Smith's admiration for Patrick Troughton's performance creep in. Although Troughton's reactions

---

[34] For example in Parkin, Lance, *Time Unincorporated: The Doctor Who Fanzine Archives* Vol 1: Lance Parkin, p140.

[35] On stage at the Edinburgh Television Festival in 2010. Smith would agree with this assessment when asked about it by Kirsty Young on **Desert Island Discs**: 'Even when I was young I looked sort of craggy'.

[36] Quoted in Spilsbury, 'The Time is Now!', p18.

[37] Smith's physicality is also repeatedly emphasised by Moffat in his 2018 novelisation of *The Day of the Doctor*, pp27, 94, 113.

are rarely overstated (large gestures would carry little impact on the smaller screens of the 1960s) he often used his hands to emphasise the nature of his lines: for instance, wringing them in a Uriah Heep manner to demonstrate his humility when gathering information from the archaeological party in *The Tomb of the Cybermen* (1967). Troughton would also tend to look for the humour in a scene (such as accidentally holding Jamie's hand entering the tomb in *Tomb*, or in chase sequences in stories such as *The Invasion* (1968) and *The Seeds of Death* (1969)): something that would fit a show being run by a writer like Moffat, with a background mainly in sitcom.

Smith's gift for physical comedy is a point of emphasis in his first episode[38]: the teaser sequence relies on it, the scenes where Amelia prepares food for him are sold by Smith's willingness to play the clown and the final confrontation with Prisoner Zero is undercut by Smith's over the top gesture when delivering the line 'Who the man?' If Smith's primary exposure to Troughton was mainly from *The Tomb of the Cybermen* he may also have realised that the comedic front presented by Troughton's Doctor is a façade for a deeper design: that the Doctor can be seen to be subtly manipulating the archaeological party in this story, with fatal consequences for several of them. The 11th Doctor, whilst ostensibly a bouncy, likeable character, can be as manipulative as Troughton in that story, particularly in instances such as his plan to cheat oblivion in *The Big Bang* (2010), his changing of Kazran Sardick's past in *A Christmas Carol* (2010), or his method for escaping the fate planned for him by the renegade Silence in *The Wedding of River Song* (2011). He is either oblivious to the emotional consequences of his actions for

---

[38] This apparently translates to the Doctor self-describing himself as an 'idiot' (Moffat, *The Day of the Doctor*, p26)

others or simply does not understand them. There are hints of this in *The Eleventh Hour*, in the way he persuades Jeff to do what he wants[39], and the way he assumes that Amy will simply accompany him at the end[40].

The Troughton influence extends beyond characterisation to elements of the costume. Smith's original costume was quite different: described by Tom Spilsbury as 'like something Captain Jack Sparrow wears in the **Pirates of the Caribbean** movies' and by Moffat as '...a bit more piratey, big long coats and all that stuff.'[41] Smith rejected it as something the Doctor would have imposed on him by others, something he would not choose for himself. Instead, his eventual look was thrown together more organically, with Smith bringing his own jacket and asking for a bow tie and braces, both of which are significant features of the second Doctor's outfit. Moffat was reluctant to add a bow tie to the costume, seeing is as 'retro,

---

[39] Jeff saving the world with a laptop thanks to the Doctor's boosting of its capabilities may be Moffat's 'fan cringe' (where fans are embarrassed about past elements of the show they did not like) in action. Mickey manages to penetrate the website of an international security organisation with a simple password in *World War Three* (2005): here, with the audience's understanding of the capabilities of the internet being more sophisticated, a less handwavey explanation is required. On the other hand, it may merely be a reference to the earlier story.

[40] He is ostensibly concerned with consequences: when asking the Atraxi what 'important' means, he prefigures his concern with every individual being important (in *A Christmas Carol* he will tell Kazran Sardick that '...in 900 years of time and space [...] I've never met anyone who wasn't important'). What separates the Doctor from the monsters for Moffat is concern for others.

[41] Troughton himself said at one point said that there was a plan to dress his Doctor as a naval captain.

outdated, ridiculous [...] a pantomime idea of what **Doctor Who**'s like'[42], but to his credit was happy to concede to his leading actor's wishes. The costume, within the fiction assembled from clothes left by doctors in a medical changing room[43], emphasises the 'mad scientist' element and perhaps the desire of the character to look older than he appears. Although it would be a categorical error to assign the Doctor an alignment on the political spectrum, the slightly old fashioned look aligns with the 'young fogey', a term applied to relatively young and generally conservative men who dress and often act in old fashioned ways[44].

Smith's costume is also an effective visual reaction against his predecessor. Tennant's costume included a fashionable suit combined with hi-top trainers[45] and often topped off with a long coat. A coat of similar length for Smith, combined with hair as fashionably extravagant as Tennant's, might not have provided as effective a visual counterpoint.

This counterpoint was important within and without the fiction: each 21st-century Doctor has to some extent been a reaction to the previous incarnation. Eccleston's short hair and Salford accent were a deliberate break from the style of his predecessors, and more

---

[42] Spilsbury, 'The Time is Now!', pp20-22. Whilst Moffat is an experienced television professional, this looks to be an example of fan cringe.

[43] Again, echoing a predecessor: Jon Pertwee's initial outfit is stolen from the changing room of a hospital, as is Paul McGann's.

[44] The term was originally coined in the 'Diary' column of *The Spectator* from 19 May 1984 by the journalist Alan Watkins.

[45] Although the BBC cannot be seen to endorse commercial brands, these are clearly based on Converse trainers.

specifically the Romantic look given to Paul McGann's Doctor[46]; Tennant was a move back to a more deliberately romantic lead; Smith would be replaced by the much older Peter Capaldi; and it hardly needs stating how Jodie Whittaker serves as a contrast to previous incarnations. Whilst Smith is not an especially obvious contrast to Tennant in terms of physique and appearance, the personality we are presented with can be seen as an obvious reaction to the 10th Doctor. Both Davies and Moffat have suggested that this is quite deliberate:

> 'we've started to suggest – I think it was Russell who started it – that the Doctor's regenerations are not completely random; he sort of alters himself with regard to the world around him.'[47]

Again, this is something that works even if it may be an explanation imposed in hindsight. The ninth Doctor is defined by survivor's guilt, a reaction to the experiences of his previous incarnation in the Time War. He is the 'coward... every time,'[48] and often leaves the crucial actions to others – Rose in his first episode, Charles Dickens in *The Unquiet Dead* (2005), Mickey in *Aliens of London* (2005) and so forth. Even towards the end of his life he cannot pull a trigger, unable to inflict capital punishment on Blon Fel Fotch Slitheen in *Boom Town* (2005) or resolve the moral dilemma of activating the delta-wave device in *The Parting of the Ways* (2005). He will not make decisions, because he is dominated by regret at the decision his previous incarnation made in ending the Time War.

---

[46] For further discussion on this, see Chapter 2 of Arnold, *Rose*.
[47] Cook, Benjamin, 'The Last Battle', DWM #521, p19.
[48] *The Parting of the Ways*.

By contrast, the 10th Doctor is more of a romantic hero: perhaps a consequence of the kiss which precipitated his regeneration. That Rose is the prime influence on his new personality is indicated by his adoption of her Estuary English accent[49]. He's also noticeably more inclined to action than his predecessor: whereas Rose's influence attempts to encourage the ninth Doctor to action, often unsuccessfully, the 10th Doctor is a more brutal proposition: after killing the Sycorax leader in *The Christmas Invasion* (2005) he describes his new personality as 'no second chances, I'm that kind of man'[50] and later observes that he '...used to have so much mercy'[51]. Whereas Rose's role with the ninth Doctor was to reconnect him to humanity, the role of the 10th Doctor's companions is to constrain him and remind him of the moral view of the less powerful. This is perhaps best demonstrated by the alternative timeline in which his hubris unchecked by Donna causes his death[52], or by the saviour complex demonstrated in *The Waters of Mars* (2009) when he has no regular companion to hold his worst impulses in check.

The 11th Doctor arrives immediately in the aftermath of the Doctor's encounter with the Time Lords in *The End of Time*, and his long goodbyes to the people important to him[53]. Although not much can be told from this brief appearance, the first noticeable change is his accent: although not using received pronunciation, Smith does not

---

[49] It may not be coincidence that the accents of Davies's Doctors reflect the primary accents of the UK's most popular soap operas.

[50] *The Christmas Invasion* (2005).

[51] *School Reunion* (2006).

[52] *Turn Left* (2008).

[53] The Doctor himself will tell us that he 'hates endings' in *The Angels Take Manhattan* (2012), another reaction which helps form his character.

adopt a regional accent as his predecessors did[54]. This cannot be seen as part of the same process by which the 10th Doctor adopted the accent of the first person he met: the first person the 11th Doctor meets is Amelia Pond and clearly he does not do a reverse Tennant and adopt a Scottish accent[55]. Accent can often be a convenient television shorthand to indicate the class of the character in question: by the end of the episode, with his more middle-class accent and dress sense, we no longer have a Doctor covering his Time Lord origin by adopting the mannerisms of the working class. Perhaps in this sense the events of *The End of Time* were somewhat cathartic for the Doctor; the encounter with the surviving Time Lords easing the guilt of his actions in the Time War and showing that he is not the sole surviving Time Lord: something exemplified by the Doctor's reply of 'I know' to Amelia telling him

---

[54] The ninth Doctor's accent is a consequence of the actor chosen for the role; the 10th Doctor's is a deliberate decision which masks David Tennant's natural Scottish accent. The novelisation of *The Christmas Invasion* suggests that the 10th Doctor picked up his accent from Rose. However, as this is part of a discussion between Rose and Mickey, whose knowledge of the regenerative process is limited, the suggestion has plausible deniability. (Colgan, Jenny, *The Christmas Invasion*, p82)

[55] Though as he is thinking about Amy when he regenerates, rather than Clara, this may explain within the fiction of the show why the 12th Doctor has a Scottish accent. (The 11th Doctor being better spoken may have to do with the last being he meets being Ood Sigma, who has a regionless accent. In other modern regenerations the last person other than himself who the War Doctor speaks to is Clara, who has a Northern accent — albeit Blackpool rather than Salford. And he in turn speaks elderly-British-actor received pronunciation, just like Ohila who was with the eighth Doctor before he regenerated.)

how lucky he is not to have an aunt. His origins and power no longer need to be concealed by shame, and the show is quite happy to emphasise how alien he is again after partially concealing it beneath Tennant's London-accented façade. The show itself is moving on from the Time War backstory of the Russell T Davies era to an ongoing, current backstory: in *The Day of the Doctor* (2013) the Moment will call the 11th Doctor the 'man who forgets', and his predecessors berate him for apparently forgetting the impact of his actions: it is a sign the show and the character have moved on[56].

This renewed emphasis on the Doctor's alien nature affects his relationship with humans: the other big difference between the 10th and the 11th Doctors is their attitude to romance. The 10th Doctor is quite happy to fraternise with other species, with a particular taste for human females: he burns up a star to say goodbye to Rose, shamelessly flirts with Madame du Pompadour (and perhaps goes further) and makes a salacious joke about Elizabeth I no longer being the 'Virgin Queen'[57]. It's this characteristic (and joke) that Steven Moffat would play up to when needing to contrast him with other incarnations in *The Day of the Doctor*. In multi-Doctor stories the

---

[56] The novelisation of *The Day of the Doctor* implies that this forgetting is not deliberate on the Doctor's part but River Song helping him to forget, pp123-24, 129.

[57] *Doomsday* (2006), *The Girl in the Fireplace* (2006) and *The End of Time* episode 1 respectively. Moffat calls back to this last line twice: in *The Beast Below* (2010) and *The Day of the Doctor*, in the latter case seemingly deliberately reasserting the 16th-century understanding of 'unmarried' rather than 'pure' over the term. The Doctor's worry follows the Queen's acceptance of his marriage proposal, not their prior romance or anything that may have happened off-screen during it.

previous Doctors are often reduced to a caricature and it's the 10th Doctor's reputation as a womaniser which makes the most effective contrast to his successor. The 10th Doctor dies having said a farewell to seemingly everyone he ever cared about: Martha, Mickey, Jack, Joan Redfern's great-granddaughter and Rose[58]: a fitting farewell for the most openly emotional of the Doctor's incarnations. By contrast the 11th Doctor comes across as almost gauche, with little or no understanding of human relationships. This is most obviously expressed in his reactions to the adult Amy: she is dressed in a kissogram policewoman outfit when he first encounters her and this does not cause him to bat an eyelid, even before he learns her true identity. He simply sees her as the same being he met as a child: 12 years is the blink of an eye to someone who at this point has lived over a thousand years, and she is still a relative child to him. Later he will reject her sexual advances and is clearly not only uncomfortable with them, but astonished that they have happened. At this point in his regeneration he is simply not interested in love or sex: again, it is dangerous to apply human terminology to a species which we subsequently know to be genderfluid, but this Doctor is, at least initially, asexual. Matt Smith would make this point in an early interview:

> 'The Doc's idea of an orgy is playing chess with an ostrich. His brain doesn't work in that way. He would find it weird and peculiar. He finds women peculiar. He is quite asexual.'[59]

---

[58] Both 10th and 11th Doctors end their lives seeing the first face that incarnation saw. The same may be true of the ninth Doctor, though it is unclear if he has met anyone or been anywhere else prior to the events seen in *Rose*.

[59] Interviewed on **Alan Carr: Chatty Man** (2009-).

He will send out mixed signals on this, particularly in regards to River Song and Tasha Lem[60], but his careless attitude to nudity in *The Time of the Doctor* (2013) indicates that this relative naivety remains a trait of this incarnation to the end. If the theory that regeneration is a reaction to the world around him holds true, this new incarnation's blind spot toward human relationships may be the regenerative process saving him from the emotional trauma of saying goodbye to loved ones for the final time[61].

The Eleventh Hour privileges us with a unique perspective: it is the first time we have seen the internal workings of the Doctor's mind[62]. The sequence on the village green with the Atraxi spaceship overhead gives us a rare insight into how the Doctor's mind works: with a deliberately overcranked frame rate and attention to minor details while everyone else is looking the other way, it shows us how an intelligence beyond our own functions. It is reminiscent of the way the shows of the **CSI** franchise treat crime scenes[63], focusing on

---

[60] His successor will imply in *Deep Breath* (2014) that these counterexamples are a form of acting out on his predecessor's part.
[61] The departure of the Ponds in *The Angels Take Manhattan* (2012) and his subsequent withdrawal from the universe as seen in *The Snowmen* (2012) indicate that, if anything, this incarnation is even less well suited to goodbyes than his predecessor.
[62] Although we have been privy to his thoughts before, via mind probes and other alien mind-reading devices in such stories as *The Space Museum* (1965) and *Day of the Daleks* (1972), during the regeneration sequences in *Logopolis* (1981) and *The Caves of Androzani* (1984), and even briefly via a voiceover in the first episode of *The Underwater Menace* (1967).
[63] It is not the only time Adam Smith will borrow a directorial technique from US shows: the scene where the Doctor and Amy discuss the time that has passed since the Doctor's first visit is

details which may be easily missed. It is also a technique this episode shares with **Sherlock**, co-created by Moffat: a visual analogue for the explanations Sherlock gives of how he solved crimes in those stories, which are often derived from the smallest details[64].

It is also important to note that the Doctor we meet here is still a developing personality – 'still cooking' as he puts it. He is in almost every scene, in direct contrast to David Tennant's introduction. Tennant's first full episode was a case of building tension until he made a heroic entrance: bar a few brief bursts of energy which help save the Tylers from menaces beyond their ability to cope with, he is incapacitated for much of the episode before making his grand entrance just in time to save the world from the Sycorax. The 11th Doctor has no such luxury: whilst 'cooking' he is obliged to investigate cracks in time, recapture an alien prisoner and save the world from destruction:

> 'A situation of escalating crisis that never allows him to sit down really... normally in **Doctor Who**, traditionally [...] the first episode of a new Doctor he has time to recover and his first instinct is to go somewhere and lie down and bring himself round. I wanted... the comedy of a man whose day just gets worse and worse and worse'[65]

---

reminiscent of the technique of exposition being delivered whilst characters are in motion characteristic of episodes of **The West Wing** directed by Thomas Schlamme.

[64] This is not the only time the shows will share storytelling techniques: for example, Moffat uses the concept of the mind palace as seen in such **Sherlock** episodes as *The Abominable Bride* (2016) in *Heaven Sent* (2015).

[65] Moffat, Steven, *The Eleventh Hour* DVD commentary.

From the Doctor's point of view, then, the events of *The Eleventh Hour* constitute a farce[66]: one crisis piling on top of another in the vein of such films as *Clockwise* (1986) or *The Hangover* (2009)[67]. This may well account for the more energetic, physical nature of this incarnation: whilst still forming he's required to expend a great deal of energy and ingenuity. The regenerative process is therefore likely to settle on this as the new normal for his new body. Given that Moffat uses the 'desktop theme' analogy when referring to the different TARDIS control rooms, perhaps the best analogy for regeneration is that each incoming Doctor's personality and appearance is akin to a newly installed operating system for a computer: although the appearance, clothes and methods differ the underlying character remains unchanged[68]. Meet the new Doctor: not quite the same as the old Doctor.

---

[66] This is essentially the point of the pre-credits sequence: it makes the point that the Doctor is off-balance from the start and having a very bad day.

[67] This accounts for the changing motivations of the Atraxi during the story: whilst Prisoner Zero is motivated by the need to escape, the Atraxi switch plans from recapture to destruction of the planet very quickly and in direct violation of laws they appear familiar with, strongly recalling a similar situation with an alien police force applying their own harsh morality to a crisis situation in *Smith and Jones* (2007). A farce requires constant escalation of crisis and this is it.

[68] 'The Doctor is the Doctor is the Doctor. It's what the new Doctor brings to it that changes the focus of the part' (Moffat, Steven, on **Toby Hadoke's Who's Round** #232). This can also be seen during the episode, occasionally repeating dialogue from the 10th Doctor, such as 'You've had some cowboys in here.' Similarly, the Doctor's climactic actions recall the resolution to *The Christmas Invasion*. This approach, of scaring aliens away with his reputation, is reused *from*

CHAPTER 2: 'THE SCOTTISH GIRL IN AN ENGLISH VILLAGE'

If the characterisation of each new Doctor can be seen as a reaction to the previous Doctor, a way to underline that the show has changed and renewed itself along with the lead actor, until 2005 the same had not been true of the role of the companion. With a few rare exceptions, the 20th-century version of the show saw the companions as almost an interchangeable plot function[69]. The role of the companion was essentially to facilitate secondary plots and allow the Doctor a foil for necessary exposition.

This changed with *Rose*, where the companion was essentially elevated to a joint leading role with the title character, most obviously expressed by the names of the actors playing both Doctor and companion appearing in the opening credits. The companion was still essentially an audience identification figure but there was an equal emphasis on her effect on the Doctor as the Doctor's effect on her. They were signified as unexceptional before their paths

---

Silence in the Library / Forest of the Dead and will be undercut when the Doctor tries repeating it a third time in *The Pandorica Opens* (2010). The trick of giving a new Doctor the old Doctor's lines and referring to recent events, to help remind an audience this is the same Doctor, is one used in both *Robot* (1974-75) and *Castrovalva*.

[69] Certainly, after Gerry Davis and Innes Lloyd altered the Doctor's role from explorer to adventurer: companions such as Barbara and Steven are allowed to become protagonists (in *The Aztecs* (1964) and *The Massacre* (1966) respectively) in a way later companions are never allowed to be. John Nathan-Turner's fondness for gimmicks (such as giving the companions different nationalities) may be seen as a way of attempting to make them distinctive from their predecessors.

crossed with the Doctor (coded with their jobs – shop assistant, junior doctor and temporary secretary[70]) before the random circumstance of a meeting with the Doctor changed their lives. The Doctor's emotional distress at their departures[71] and subsequent last goodbye just prior to regeneration[72] showed that their departures affected him in a way that they generally did not in the 20th-century series[73]. This critical element was emphasised by their first stories as regular companions[74] all placing them as the viewpoint character.

In its presentation of the new companion, then, *The Eleventh Hour* is a remarkably conventional episode. The manner in which it introduces her however, is not. While Steven Moffat was primarily considered a sitcom writer prior to beginning work on **Doctor Who**, there was more to his career. Although he had mainly worked on

---

[70] This even extends to Mickey, who works in a garage (*The Christmas Invasion*), Astrid, who is a waitress, and Wilf, who apparently keeps himself busy in his later years by selling newspapers at night (*Voyage of the Damned* (2007)).

[71] In *Doomsday, Last of the Time Lords* (2007) and *Journey's End* respectively

[72] *The End of Time* episode 2.

[73] Although certain departures are played out as having an emotional impact (such as Susan in *The Dalek Invasion of Earth* (1964) and Jo in *The Green Death* (1973)), the nature of the 20th-century series as essentially an anthology series linked by main characters means little time is given to reflection on the companions' impact on the Doctor: the Doctor's soliloquy at the conclusion of *The Massacre* is a rare example, with perhaps only the faces appearing during *The Caves of Androzani* having a similar effect. The most egregious example of the Doctor moving on quickly is the swift dismissal of Adric's death in *Time-Flight* (1982).

[74] *Rose, Smith and Jones* (2007) and *Partners in Crime* (2008).

sitcoms in the 1990s and early 2000s (**Joking Apart** (1991-95), **Chalk** (1997) and **Coupling** (2000-04), as well as three episodes of Dawn French's **Murder Most Horrid** (1994-99)), his career had begun with the children's series **Press Gang**, which dealt sensitively with subject matter such as child abuse[75] and teen suicide[76]. It would be equally accurate – more so after his time on **Doctor Who** – to paint Moffat as a writer of romances.

Of the series he created, **Press Gang**, **Joking Apart** and **Coupling** were each driven by romantic relationships in differing stages. Similarly, with the exception of *Blink*, his **Doctor Who** episodes under Russell T Davies had emphasised the Doctor's relationships with human women: *The Empty Child / The Doctor Dances* (2005) tested the Ninth Doctor and Rose's relationship by adding a wild card in Captain Jack, building on the suggestion in *Doctor Who* (1996) that he could be a romantic hero; *The Girl in the Fireplace* (2006) apparently featured him falling in love with Madame du Pompadour, and *Silence in the Library / Forest of the Dead* (2008) introduced the Doctor's future wife. With this in mind it's no surprise that the core element Moffat drew from his predecessor was an emphasis on the Doctor-companion relationship as the key to the show, rather than the conflict between the Doctor and family[77].

---

[75] **Press Gang**: *Something Terrible* (two episodes, 1990).

[76] **Press Gang**: *How to Make a Killing* (two episodes, 1989) and *Monday - Tuesday* (1989).

[77] Davies and Moffat parallel each other in the relationships their companions have with the Doctor: their first companion is, at least initially, romantically attracted to him, their second is also romantically interested but the feeling is not reciprocated, and their

The role played by family is one of the major differences between Davies's and Moffat's versions of the show. Whilst Moffat has rightly pointed out that to define either version of the modern show as reductively as 'kitchen sink' or 'fairytale' is a 'grotesque exaggeration'[78], there's a kernel of truth at the heart of both descriptions. In interviews immediately after departing the series, Moffat described the show as essentially about 'a wizard in a magic box with a magic wand'[79].

Davies's version of the show takes the trouble to give each companion a fully fleshed-out background which wouldn't be out of place in dramatic genres which aspire to realism: the families of Rose, Martha and Donna all play significant roles in the seasons in which they appear. They act as a domestic anchor to ground the more fantastical elements of the series and remain an important part of the companions' lives, even when travelling with the Doctor offers the escape the companion thinks they want. Each companion's mother in particular is concerned with the consequences of their child travelling with the Doctor[80], and each of them is used to emphasise alien invasions disrupting everyday life[81].

---

third companion is not interested in anything but a platonic friendship.

[78] 'Steven Moffat on Matt Smith's Era, Writing the 50th Anniversary and **More**'.

[79] Both in 'Steven Moffat on Matt Smith's Era, Writing the 50th Anniversary and **More**' and in **Toby Hadoke's Who's Round** #232.

[80] In the case of Francine Jones this extends to betraying the Doctor and her daughter to the Master (*42*, *The Sound of Drums* (both 2007)).

[81] Amongst other instances, Jackie is threatened by the Autons in *Rose* and the Slitheen in *Aliens of London / World War Three* (2005), Martha's family are captured and subjugated by the Master in *The*

Davies's version of the show views travelling with the Doctor as the equivalent of sowing wild oats: irresponsible, carefree adventures of youth before settling down into an adult world of commitment. Rose, Mickey, Martha and Donna all end up married off in conventional fashion and even the omnisexual Jack appears to find a Doctor-approved partner: Davies's idea of a happy ending is the companion walking off into the sunset holding hands with their loved one[82].

By contrast the role of the family is significantly reduced in Moffat's version of the show, something evident from the first scenes of *The Eleventh Hour* onwards. The opening montage of *Rose* deliberately establishes Rose's domestic routine: living arrangements, boyfriend and job. By contrast, after the familiar zoom in from outer space to open the episode, Moffat chooses to try to intrigue the audience rather than comfort them, emphasising the oddness of Amelia's life[83]. Our first meeting with Amelia has a slightly off-key feel compared to the series under Davies: although Aunt Sharon is mentioned in her prayer to Santa[84], there is a striking absence of

---

Sound of Drums / Last of the Time Lords (2007) and Sylvia and Wilf are threatened by Daleks in *The Stolen Earth / Journey's End* and the Master in *The End of Time*.

[82] The only character who does not receive an explicitly happy ending is the 10th Doctor, who regenerates railing against the dying of the light. By contrast the other 21st-century Doctors have seemingly ended their time fulfilled and without regrets.

[83] In keeping with the series' approach, in this book 'Amelia' will be used to refer to the character as a child and 'Amy' as the adult.

[84] Aunt Sharon will not appear until the final episode of the season, *The Big Bang*.

adult figures aside from the Doctor, and we will not meet any other members of the Pond family until *The Big Bang*.

The TARDIS' crashing and demolition of the shed, the Doctor's subsequent sampling of various foods and his investigation of the crack in Amy's bedroom wall are hardly scenes conducive to anyone in the vicinity sleeping: it is somewhat strange that Amelia's aunt has left her alone and travelled far enough away at night that she is completely oblivious as to what might happen to Amelia[85]. As a result, the Amelia we meet is a lonely child, essentially a foundling, living in a house under threat from forces incomprehensible to her[86]: her response to the Doctor's initial offer to travel with him is therefore entirely understandable. Instantly, he is the key adult figure in her life, offering a kind of security in times of trouble, whereas under Davies he was a disruptive force tempting the companions away from their family and friends.

This introduction mirrors Moffat's earlier story *The Girl in the Fireplace* – both feature the Doctor meeting a young girl and discovering the monsters in their bedroom are real, then returning years later to discover that the girl has grown into a young woman with a fascination with him. In both cases the relationship with the Doctor is presented as the central relationship of the character's life, despite what history tells us about Madame de Pompadour[87]. Whilst

---

[85] Particularly given that this initial meeting is apparently set in 1996, when mobile phones were relatively uncommon.

[86] Reflected in the shots immediately following the opening credits: the wind moving a child's handheld windmill toy and a garden swing.

[87] The differences between the stories are fundamentally of tone: *The Girl in the Fireplace* is a tragic romance whereas *The Eleventh*

parents are not relevant to the story in *The Girl in the Fireplace*, in *The Eleventh Hour* they are a part of the mystery relating to the season arc which will not be explicitly mentioned or resolved until the series finale[88]. The exclusive focus on the Doctor and his companion marks this out as a very different version of the show. With the Doctor not representing an escape from mundane existence, the motivations for Amy eventually accompanying him are very different: he represents the wonder and security of childhood, rather than the misadventures of late youth.

The Doctor's accidental abandonment of Amelia, combined with her parents being 'eaten' by the crack in time, therefore leaves her with the absence of a father figure. Abandonment by a male figure is a recurring theme in the 21st-century series, and it is usually marked by the Doctor acting as a surrogate figure to his companions. Rose's father is dead; Martha's parents are divorced; production circumstances see Donna's father die offscreen between *The*

Hour is essentially the same story played as a farce with a happy ending.

[88] At this point it's tempting to speculate that Amy's aunt is also eaten by the cracks at some point. This does leave the question of Amy's upbringing: the story implies that Amy remains resident in her house with Prisoner Zero, saying that it has had 'years' to obtain Amy's imprint, and yet there is no indication from other characters in the village of an unusual situation. The question as to how the cracks work in leaving descendants behind while absorbing their parents is, for storytelling purposes, probably best left vague.

Runaway Bride and *Partners in Crime*[89]; and Bill is a foster child[90]. At the time of writing, Amy is the sole companion of the modern series to have no apparent relationship with her parents at all. Even when they are restored to existence by the events of The *Big Bang*, they are narratively unimportant aside from indicating that the universe is running as it was before the cracks existed[91].

It is a sign that family relationships are less important to Moffat's vision of the show[92]. Instead the important relationships for Moffat era companions are romantic ones. Whereas Rose and Donna are forced from the TARDIS by circumstance, and Martha leaves of her own volition, the essential choice for Moffat's companions when deciding whether to leave the TARDIS is between the Doctor and a lover: Amy and Rory, Clara and Danny, Bill and Heather. With Smith deciding that his Doctor was essentially asexual, this emphasis on adult relationships allowed Moffat to retain the element of

---

[89] Due to the death of actor Howard Attfield. Within the fiction this is a possible motivation for her decision to change her mind about travelling with the Doctor.

[90] Clara is the exception to this rule, having instead lost her mother relatively young but still being on good enough terms with her father and stepmother to invite them round for Christmas dinner in *The Time of the Doctor*.

[91] Augustus and Tabetha Pond appear only in *The Big Bang* and the tie-in novel *Borrowed Time* (2011) by Naomi Alderman.

[92] At times this may also make this version of the show less 'realistic': the families of Moffat-era companions simply serve the story when they do appear. We do not see, for example, the effects of their eventual fates on their families, and with no emotional resonance the companions during the Moffat era may seem less convincing. In this respect it is something of a shame that the 'PS' minisode which showed the Doctor and Brian Pond dealing with the consequences of Amy and Rory's fate was never fully made.

relationship comedies that have largely been his stock in trade as a writer outside of his work on **Doctor Who**[93].

This shift in emphasis is part of the changed nature of the Doctor: this new Doctor does not view humans as a moral conscience nor potential love interests, but instead as 'strange, alien.'[94] He therefore does not allow them to accompany him because of who they are, but because of a mystery connected with them, a pattern that holds true for each of the female companions of the Moffat era. His connection with them is, at least initially, intellectual. The final moments of *The Eleventh Hour* make it clear that the mystery of the cracks in time plays a large part in his decision to take Amy on board the TARDIS[95]. We do see mysteries develop around Rose (the Bad Wolf arc) and Donna (the prophecies of the Ood and Dalek Sec), but these play no part in their being invited on board the TARDIS. By contrast the mysteries surrounding Amy and Clara identify them as already special: there are circumstances which mark them out as above ordinary people. Combined with their introductions, which show them as something out of the ordinary (in Amy's case 'the Scottish girl in the English village'), this could be seen as another

---

[93] As Smith's Doctor develops he does become more flirtatious, particularly with River Song and with Tasha Lem (*The Time of the Doctor* (2013)), but his early appearances display a notable awkwardness around women displaying a physical interest in him, particularly Amy and River in *The Time of Angels / Flesh and Stone* (2010).

[94] Smith, Matt, in **Doctor Who Confidential**: *Call Me the Doctor* (2010).

[95] Similarly, he is curious about the multiple iterations of Clara, and Bill's initial involvement with the Doctor comes about due to a mysterious puddle.

factor making them harder to relate to than the companions of the Davies era.

This attitude of the Doctor to his companions springs from Moffat's basic conception of the show. He has repeatedly stated that **Doctor Who** is a children's show, and his idea of the role of the companions arises from that:

> 'it's a children's programme. And, explicitly the companions are Doctor Who's children... They're in his care, and lovely old Doctor Who is opening the TARDIS doors and saying "I will always look after you". Get it right – that's the story.'[96]

Whilst this raises disturbing questions about the attempted seduction at the end of *Flesh and Stone*[97] it explains more clearly the Doctor's relationship with his companions in the Moffat era, which is not a meeting of ostensible equals with a hint of romance, as was the case under Davies[98], but a patriarchal one. Fundamentally the Doctor is the senior figure in the relationship, in terms of both age and authority. In the early stages of the arcs of both season 5 and 6 he keeps a secret from his companions (the nature of the cracks and the indeterminate readings regarding Amy's pregnancy) and he often acts manipulatively (such as the consequences of Rory's death in *Cold Blood* (2010)). Taking them on board the TARDIS is a

---

[96] Moffat, Steven, DWM #515, September 2017, p14

[97] It can be seen as an explicit onscreen rejection of the relatively overtly sexualised portrayal of the Doctor during the Russell T Davies years: in many ways this Doctor is a child too.

[98] The trailer for series 3, for instance, involves a split screen shot of the Doctor and Martha which visually suggests equality, and the arc of series 4 involves what the Ood call the 'Doctor-Donna', implying an inseparable partnership.

protective gesture, keeping them safe from something he cannot explain and they cannot deal with as mere humans.

Extending this metaphor further, like any child Amy is not above keeping secrets from the Doctor when she feels it necessary – sometimes to save herself embarrassment, such as the revelations of her childhood stories about the 'raggedy Doctor' and, initially, that she is due to be married the day after the Doctor finally takes her on board the TARDIS. At least to begin with, this is a relationship founded on secrecy and deception, with Amy allowing the promise of her childhood dreams to override the responsibility of staying and preparing for her wedding. It's an immature but understandable choice, which indicates that she's still a child at heart. Along with her job as a kissogram and attempted seduction of the Doctor, it also suggests that there is something unfulfilling in her relationship with Rory at this point – initially at least he is clearly a Doctor substitute, with Amy having him dress up as the 'raggedy Doctor' in childhood games and pushing him into a medical career[99].

From what we see in 2008 it is clear that, for all that Amy is engaged in a long-term romantic relationship, the Doctor is still the key figure in her life. A running gag in the episode is how the Doctor is familiar to the inhabitants of Leadworth through Amy's obsession with him: Mrs Angelo, Jeff and Rory all recognise the Doctor from the games, cartoons and dolls Amy created in the wake of their first encounter. Amy can therefore be read as the first fan to journey in the

---

[99] Deleted dialogue from the episode suggests he initially looked to train to be a doctor, but became a nurse when it became clear that his original career path was impractical.

TARDIS[100]. This is not to say she is uncritical of the Doctor – far from it, as her reactions to his return after several years show, she is not afraid to call him out when she perceives he has done wrong[101].

This distinguishes her from Elton Pope in *Love & Monsters* (2006), who is more trusting and uncritical, partially explaining why the Doctor does not invite him in but later invites Amy. Indeed, much as the structure of the episode owes an admitted debt to *The Girl in the Fireplace* it can also be described as *Love & Monsters* with a happy ending. Both Elton and Amelia lose their parents early on to an alien incursion involving the Doctor, and in both cases this results in a lifelong obsession and admiration for him which helps build an indulgent community around them. Elton, however, does not appear to develop the independent turn of mind Amy does – much of his existence appears to be bedroom-bound and the encounter with the Hoix terrifies him. Amy, in contrast, develops enough self-confidence to pursue a career as a kissogram and form healthy adult relationships.

This relative self-confidence is also a move away from the character flaws of the Davies companions. They need the Doctor as a route out of the drudgery of their everyday existence: the urban routine of getting up and going out to work and watching television with a

---

[100] For those who like meta readings of texts, it may be significant that Amelia meets the Doctor briefly in 1996 and waits years for his reappearance while filling the gap with creating her own toys and stories.

[101] These include both scenes where the Doctor returns after a gap of several years and the key scene where Amy shuts the Doctor's tie in a car door and demands an explanation, despite a clear alien threat which only the Doctor can deal with.

takeaway in the evening. Even for Martha, the most independent of the companions, it's an escape from the bickering of separated parents. Amy is a deliberate contrast to this. Where Rose and Martha both accept the invitation to travel with the Doctor after their initial adventure with him, and Donna quickly changes her mind, Amy is far more self-sufficient – a conscious choice in both the writing and playing of the character. The structure of the episode forces this on the character: she is initially apparently abandoned by the Doctor for 12 years[102], and then for a further two years after the events of the main body of the episode. Amy cannot get instant gratification as Davies's companions could; instead she has to construct a life and live it without the Doctor around. While this manifests itself in her essentially becoming a fan, the more domestic elements we do not see emphasise her relative self-sufficiency; whilst always having a certain fixation with the 'raggedy man' (as apparently having to see four psychiatrists indicates) she gets on with life:

'Amy's not going to mope around when the Doctor's not there – she's going to do her own thing.'[103]

By the time we meet Amy as an adult she has put in place the basis of her adult life: a job and a long-term relationship. The notion of becoming a kissogram in a small village where much of the community appear to know each other is certainly an enterprising one[104], and indicates a certain lack of embarrassment, but may also

---

[102] This will later be shown to not quite be the case (*The Angels Take Manhattan*).
[103] Gillan, Karen, quoted in Mulkern, Patrick and Mark Braxton, *Radio Times: Doctor Who – The Companions*, p14.
[104] *The Vampires of Venice* (2010) shows that there are at least two people in this line of trade in Leadworth.

be influenced by Amy's childhood love of dressing up: perhaps one of the more unusual influences the Doctor has had on anyone.

Amy's independence is also emphasised by Karen Gillan's choices in how to play her. Gillan was seeking to subvert the idea of the companion somewhat: whereas Rose, Donna and Martha were dazzled to some extent, Amy's years of waiting have left her with a more sceptical attitude towards the Doctor, a less trusting one than if she had been able to accompany him when he first turned up.

'She's quite a feisty girl. Amy's not so much in awe of the Doctor... she doesn't just listen to any old rubbish...'

The closest antecedent to Amy, like so much of Moffat's version of the series, comes from the early 1980s with her mirror-image, Tegan – another character seen to be repeatedly let down by the Doctor and not averse to questioning and criticising him. Both are part of the periodic deliberate departures from what Gillan terms the 'whole, likeable, girl-next-door business'[105] perhaps best exemplified by 1970s companions Jo Grant and Sarah Jane Smith.

Whereas Amy is clearly presented as the main companion, with the episode's story essentially being how she comes to travel with the Doctor, in this first episode Rory appears at best to be a subsidiary character, a minor theme in the Doctor and Amy's story. His first scene is low key, simple exposition setting up the mystery of the coma patients[106] and we do not learn of his significance until the

---

[105] Mulkern and Braxton, *The Companions*, p19.
[106] This raises the question of how often Prisoner Zero has been sneaking off into Leadworth to gain a new body imprint. It also raises the mystery of how Doctor is unfamiliar with the then-common technology of a camera on a mobile phone.

Doctor notices him on the village green pointing his cameraphone at a person rather than the giant Atraxi spaceship overhead. He appears to become involved almost by chance, before abruptly being introduced as Amy's fiancé. At this point he seems to be a comic character much in the vein of Mickey in the show's first season: the long-term partner representing domesticity that the putative companion will inevitably throw over for a life of excitement and adventure with the Doctor. Initially his relationship with Amy appears rather convenient: a way for the Doctor to link the mystery of the coma patients with the crack in the wall and Prisoner Zero.

This plot convenience would have been smoothed over somewhat by the deleted dialogue which revealed that Amy encouraged him to pursue a career as a doctor to fulfil her obsession, imprinting him as a substitute for the raggedy Doctor. It's a shame that this dialogue was lost as it elegantly sketches in detail about Rory's character and his relationship with Amy: he cannot live up to the impossible ideal of the Doctor in Amy's head, but loves her enough to try as hard as he can. This would have neatly prefigured their eventual relationship, where he spends 2,000 years guarding her and, with the Doctor's assistance, blowing up a Cyberfleet in pursuit of a simple clue as to where kidnappers have taken her[107]. Without these lines, the impression of convenience is not dispelled until the very last shot of the episode. After Amy has accepted the Doctor's invitation we see Amy's wedding dress – clearly the intervening years between the Doctor's visits have rendered him more important to her than we might initially think. Rory will represent

---

[107] *The Big Bang, A Good Man Goes to War* (2011).

Amy's dilemma over travelling with the Doctor to their very last episode, when ultimately she chooses him over the Doctor.

At the end of *The Eleventh Hour* she chooses the TARDIS over the wedding dress; her departure is triggered, and her maturity signified, by that choice being reversed. She chooses the reality of life with Rory over a fairy-tale life with the Doctor.

CHAPTER 3: THE SCOTTISH BOY IN A WELSH CITY

Steven Moffat's acceptance of the executive producer role often designated as 'showrunner' on **Doctor Who** marked the first time that a writer or producer had taken an apparently backward career step to accept such a role. At the time of taking over, Moffat had written the primetime BBC drama **Jekyll** (2007), was contracted as a writer of a planned series of **Tintin** films and, alongside Mark Gatiss, had pitched the idea for a modern Sherlock Holmes series to the BBC. Taking the role of **Doctor Who** showrunner would mean he would have to give up a more lucrative role in the American film industry for a role in television which, for all **Doctor Who**'s undoubted success under Russell T Davies, was both less prestigious and less lucrative.

His career is one of the more remarkable of any British television writer: bar one episode of **Stay Lucky** (1989-93), three of Dawn French vehicle **Murder Most Horrid** and **Doctor Who**, Moffat's work has entirely been on shows he has created or fully authored. Moffat's initial break was the result of an exceptional stroke of luck. His father, Bill Moffat, was the headmaster of Thorn Primary School. When it was used for the production of an episode of **Highway** (1983-93), he mentioned to the producers that he had an idea for a series about a school newspaper. He had no interest in a career as a scriptwriter and sold the idea on condition that his son write a sample script. It is worth noting at this point that this was not in any way nepotistic: if the scripts had not been good enough then the production team could have declined them. If they were good then they would have a writer on board at a relatively low cost:

'She (Sandra C Hastie, **Press Gang**'s producer) sort of sighed and said "Oh god I'll read it once, I'm not paying for it obviously but I'll read one script from him and then I'll get a proper writer." So, I sent in a script and she loved it. And with that kind of incredible sort of madness-cum-genius of the woman, says I immodestly, she just decided that I'd write the whole series. Out of nowhere, out of a school in Greenock longing to be a writer I just suddenly was with my own television show.'

This is a slight exaggeration of events – as Moffat himself admits in the commentary[108], this was the version he had recited for so long as anecdote he no longer remembered whether it was true or false. A neophyte television writer suddenly having their own show is a situation extremely rare then and unthinkable today.

Press Gang ran successfully for five series between 1989 and 1993 and followed the adventures of a group of pupils asked to run a young person's version of a local newspaper, the *Junior Gazette*. Most notably the unquestioned lead character of the series was female: Lynda Day as played by Julia Sawalha. Moffat called her the character who was most fun to write and got most of the plots moving[109]. She might be best summed up as a youthful version of a career woman, initially described by Moffat as 'evil' but amended to 'amoral'. The heart of the series would be her on-off relationship with American pupil James 'Spike' Thomson. Even in his earliest days as a television writer, there is a clear style forming, with much of their dialogue being fast, witty, quippy and full of one-liners. This is

---

[108] Moffat, Steven, DVD commentary for the **Press Gang** episode *Breakfast at Czar's* (1990).
[109] Moffat, *Breakfast at Czar's* commentary.

a relatively unusual style for British comedy writers, more in the vein of American comedy[110]. According to the show's fanzine this was no accident:

> 'Steven Moffat, when writing the first season's scripts, asked his pupils what TV programmes they watched. He discovered that their favourite programmes were American imports like **Cheers, Moonlighting, Hill Street Blues** and **St Elsewhere**. "In other words," claimed Steven, "all the things I watch, so that's the audience I've written for."'[111]

This aspect won him praise from the show's cast: 'he can just throw them (one-liners) off the top of his head and they're funny every time.'[112]

Lynda and Spike are archetypes of the romantic characters Moffat would come to write: Lynda is omnicompetent and often frustrated and exasperated with Spike while Spike is somewhat more feckless,

---

[110] This style may be a reason why Moffat's version of **Doctor Who** is the most successful version in the USA: the humour is perhaps more familiar to them than the often slapstick comedy of Russell T Davies. It might also be telling of the increasing influence on a UK audience of US imports from the early 1980s.

[111] O'Brien, Steve, 'Picking Up the Pieces', *Breakfast at Czar's* #1, p8. All these series are set in the North-East of America. When Moffat was asked for influences onstage at the San Diego Comic Con in 2016, the only non-**Doctor Who** writer he specifically cited as a 'comedy god' was New York-born playwright Neil Simon. It's hard not to conclude that Moffat's writing style is broadly more influenced by the comedy of the East Coast of America than anything produced in the UK.

[112] Fletcher, Dexter, in an unfinished 'Making of Press Gang' documentary included on **Press Gang**: *The Complete Series 2* DVDs.

preferring to wing it rather than prepare for a situation[113]. That many of Moffat's characters are archetypes does not mean they are the same character: rather their natures are templates within which the details may be very different[114]. Moffat's success at writing a show with a strong female lead character whose life was not necessarily driven by romance led Sandra Hastie to note that he was a 'marvellously non-sexist writer.' Indeed, his motivation for writing such a strong female lead gives the lie to charges of sexism and misogyny made during his time on **Doctor Who**[115]:

> 'I've never been a 17-year-old girl. It's rather interesting to think like one or to force yourself to consider the world from that perspective [...] it actually started to make me a bit angry from time to time [...] I never really thought about it before [...] you consider the world from this highly dynamic, highly talented 17-year-old girl thinking what's going to happen to her, thinking how much harder it's going to be for her than it would have been if she'd been a boy. It made me very angry.'[116]

---

[113] Notably though, he is not as submissive as, for instance, the leads in **Coupling**.

[114] On stage at the Gallifrey One convention in 2018, for instance, Moffat made it clear that he did not always write the same female character, citing for instance the differences between Missy, River Song and Clara.

[115] For instance: Romana, Aja, 'Why does the Man Behind **Doctor Who** and **Sherlock** still have a job?'; Stavri, Zoe, 'Irene Adler: How to Butcher a Brilliant Woman Character'; and Jones, Jane Clare, 'Is **Sherlock** Sexist? Steven Moffat's Wanton Women'.

[116] Moffat, Steven, unfinished 'Making of Press Gang' documentary.

Moffat's identification with the plight of his lead character and anger that she would be held back simply because of gender are certainly not the words of a nascent misogynist: if anything they're entirely the opposite. This is an attitude which has not changed over the years. Although his subsequent authored series featured male leads[117] he has at least attempted to demonstrate female characters are their equal or better: Susan and Sally hold down successful careers in **Coupling**; **Sherlock** (as in the original short story 'A Scandal in Bohemia') is outwitted by Irene Adler, and the villain behind the events of that show's fourth series is Sherlock and Mycroft's even smarter sister, Eurus. In the case of **Doctor Who**, this is taken to the point of being accused of making the companion the Doctor's equal or better[118]. In a convention panel Moffat would say that misogyny was 'a genuine force for evil in the world' and 'a serious and deadly disease'[119]. His female characters may be as flawed as his male characters, but without flaws there would be no engine for drama or comedy.

Press Gang would also showcase other elements of Moffat's style which would become familiar: a willingness to indulge in non-linear storytelling (*Monday–Tuesda*y (1989)), a blurring of the lines between fantasy and reality (*Day Dreams* (1992), *UnXpected* (1992),

---

[117] Although he can hardly be blamed for Tom Jackman (the Henry Jekyll figure in **Jekyll**), Sherlock Holmes, Dracula or the Doctor being male leads.

[118] For instance, Shulz, Kyle Robert, 'The Overexposure of Clara Oswald'. This view neglects that Russell T Davies had effectively made the companion the Doctor's equal in his first season, and the names of the actors playing the Doctor and his companion have been a fixture of the opening titles since *Rose*.

[119] Onstage at the Gallifrey One convention in 2018.

There Are Crocodiles (1993)) and Moffat's penchant for in-jokes. As well as taking things Sandra C Hastie had said in the production office and giving them as dialogue to Lynda, the episode *UnXpected* would feature a show 'Colonel X', an episode where the character Frazz watched episodes of a recently cancelled genre television series for an anniversary retrospective. The eponymous Colonel was played by a former Doctor[120] and the show appeared to have the level of effects work commensurate with **Doctor Who**'s in the 1980s.

Although **Press Gang** won a BAFTA and a Royal Television Society award it ended after the fifth series when ITV informed production company Richmond Films that 'they felt it had 'outgrown its Children's ITV slot' and ratings had fallen. This also led to the cancellation of the 90-minute television film *Dead Line*, cited by Steve O'Brien in the **Press Gang** fanzine as a 'dark and sinister' story which seemed to 'round off **Press Gang** in its present format, and with an ending that actually surprised' him[121].

Moffat's major sitcom work of the 1990s would be drawn from his own experience, almost an exercise in writing what you know. **Joking Apart**, which was produced contemporaneously with later seasons of **Press Gang**, drew on Moffat's recent divorce to the point of using lines he and his ex-wife had exchanged. Again, it often indulged in fantasy sequences, with a major part of the show being the lead character, a comedy writer, commentating on the action via imaginary stand-up routines. **Chalk**, Moffat's first sitcom for BBC1 set in a school, and **Coupling** would both draw on Moffat's new relationship.

---

[120] Michael Jayston. Yes, the Valeyard counts.
[121] O'Brien, Steve, 'Stop Press', *Breakfast at Czar's* #1, p4.

1996 saw Moffat's first official association with **Doctor Who**[122], writing the short story 'Continuity Errors' for the Virgin Publishing anthology *Decalog 3: Consequences*. It's a story featuring the seventh Doctor and literary companion Bernice Summerfield set in a library containing 'any book of any type written in all of history, in all the known Universe'[123]. It features non-linear storytelling, one apparently unconnected strand of the story as a comment on another, a strong female antagonist with a line in pithy put-downs and the Doctor resolving a crisis by fiddling with the past until an implacable opponent (in this case an intransigent librarian) is willing to give him what he needs to resolve the crisis[124]. It also features the question of whether the Doctor is a good man[125] and the notion that 'monsters have nightmares' about him[126]. In retrospect it's a story which both breaks the show's format entirely and is a very good pointer to the motifs Moffat would bring to the show.

The seventh Doctor of the Virgin Publishing era was, building on hints from the television series, happy to meddle in history to get his own way[127]. The implication of Moffat's story – much as when he

---

[122] It may be no coincidence that the Doctor's initial encounter with Amy is in 1996, his second in 2008 when Moffat was asked to take over the show and the third and final visit when the Doctor and Amy finally travel together, in 2010, when the first episode of his era aired.

[123] Moffat, Steven, 'Continuity Errors', in Lane, Andy, and Justin Richards, eds, *Decalog 3: Consequences*, p218. This premise may seem familiar.

[124] And this.

[125] Moffat, 'Continuity Errors', p221.

[126] Moffat, 'Continuity Errors', p228.

[127] The best example of this is the 'War' trilogy of books by Andrew Cartmel (*Cat's Cradle: Warhead* (1992), *Warlock* (1995) and

repeated the same idea later with a different Doctor – is that the Doctor is essentially invincible, as he will happily get round any problem by simply going back and preventing it from arising in the first place. This immediately drains any situation of jeopardy: a fundamental problem in a time-travel adventure series. The only thing preventing the Doctor from becoming a monster dominating the universe and changing it to suit his whims is his own morality[128].

All this is pointed out in the segments consisting of Professor Candy's lecture notes, which question the Doctor's nature while also being essential to the comedy of the piece. It is, essentially, the Moffat era in miniature: a light, funny time-travel adventure which under the surface has extremely bleak implications. Moffat would also write a short story for Big Finish's first short story collection *Bernice Summerfield and the Dead Men Diaries* (2000), the sole work he would undertake for the licensed spinoff company[129]. As with 'Continuity Errors' it features non-linear storytelling and uses academic observations to commentate on the main action, which

---

Warchild (1996)), which constitute a longitudinal study of the Doctor's manipulative nature and its long-term consequences.

[128] This may, as a by-product, explain why the Time Lords initially look on renegades with such disfavour: the understanding of the consequences the actions of a being with the power to alter history may have. Their stance seems noticeably more relaxed once they have taken to nudging history using the Doctor as an agent (*Colony in Space* (1971), *The Curse of Peladon* (1972), *The Mutants* (1972) and *Genesis of the Daleks* (1975)).

[129] He was invited to write for Big Finish when they first acquired their **Doctor Who** licence, but declined as they did not have the right to the then current Doctor, Paul McGann, and this was the only Doctor he had an interest in writing for (Cook, Benjamin, *Doctor Who: The New Audio Adventures – The Inside Story*, p13).

features a **Blake's 7** fan becoming one of the most important men in history and ends with that series being regarded as the 26th-century equivalent of a literary classic. Again, this is an early example of the theme of people being remembered long after their time[130].

His next **Doctor Who** work was the Comic Relief special *The Curse of Fatal Death*, broadcast as two segments on Comic Relief night in 1999. This reunited Moffat with **Press Gang** star Julia Sawalha and featured Rowan Atkinson as the Doctor and Jonathan Pryce as the Master. Again, there is a sequence based around the idea of the Doctor going back and amending history to foil a villain's plans and a willingness to play with the format of the show under cover of comedy. It portrays the Master as an incompetent pantomime villain (failing to turn off his microphone when gloating about his plans for the Doctor), the notion of the Doctor getting married[131] and his retirement[132], a character aging centuries offscreen whilst little time passes for others[133], a redeemed Master[134], risqué jokes[135], obscure continuity references[136], the notion that the Doctor makes it safe to be scared, and a male-to-female regeneration[137]. What might, in lesser hands, have simply been an excuse for cheap fun at the show's

---

[130] This forms the crux of Moffat's final episode, *Twice Upon a Time*.
[131] Cf *The Wedding of River Song*.
[132] Cf *The Snowmen*.
[133] Cf *The Time of the Doctor*.
[134] Cf *World Enough and Time / The Doctor Falls*.
[135] The sonic screwdriver apparently has **three** settings. Moffat is certainly not misogynistic but it is possible to see how a penchant for sexual humour may look like sexism.
[136] The adventure takes place on Tersurus, named in *The Deadly Assassin* (1976) as the planet on which Chancellor Goth apparently found the dying Master.
[137] Prophetically, a blonde 13th Doctor.

expense is instead a loving homage to the series which, as with the ending of *Survival* (1989), sees the Doctor walking off to new adventures. As with 'Continuity Errors' it has the feeling of Moffat using all the **Doctor Who** ideas he wants to play with just in case he never has the chance to use them again[138].

Later that year Moffat was asked to take part in a DWM feature attempting to imagine a place for the series in the 21st century; an ambitious proposition given that the first attempt at a revival had led nowhere. It's a remarkable piece, in which five of the six writers involved went on to write for the 21st century show, with two running it. While he does not tempt fate in the manner of Russell T Davies ('God help anyone in charge of bringing it back')[139], there is an observation which is key to how Moffat would eventually shape the show when he had creative charge of it:

> 'The core elements are a Police Box, a frock coat and cliffhangers [...] I'd chuck out all gratuitous continuity because it's dull [...] I don't care where the Doctor comes from or why he travels the universe. I just want him out of those TARDIS doors and having adventures. Us kids want Narnia, not the wardrobe.'[140]

---

[138] In retrospect it's a good practice run for a decade later instead. Moffat even goes so far as to reuse the line 'I've put a lot of work into it' in *The Eleventh Hour*, although it's scaled down from talking about the universe to talking about the Earth. He also reuses the 'look after the universe' quote verbatim in the Karn prologue to *The Magician's Apprentice*.

[139] Quoted in Gillat, Gary, 'We're Gonna Be Bigger than **Star Wars**!', DWM #279, p12.

[140] Quoted in Gillat, 'Bigger than **Star Wars**!', p11.

The manifesto was clear: a Steven Moffat version of **Doctor Who** would above all be designed to appeal to children and grown-up children.

CHAPTER 4: 'BIT FAIRYTALE...'

'I think it's the single best children's show ever made – the funniest, the cleverest, the sweetest, the scariest – and all in all too much fun to ever grow out of.'

[Steven Moffat][141]

In interviews conducted after he had left the post of **Doctor Who** showrunner, Steven Moffat railed against the reductive descriptions applied to their versions of the show:

'Russell and I, in order to make us look different, have to be caricatured in our approaches [...] I think that most people who are not **Doctor Who** fans, if you described the first four years of **Doctor Who** as a kitchen sink drama would be wondering what the hell was in your kitchen [...] that's a grotesque exaggeration, and the fairytale approach is a grotesque exaggeration of mine really.'[142]

That this description is one which has stuck after eight years shows how successful this description was in attempting to differentiate Davies's and Moffat's versions of the show. Moffat would subsequently dismiss this as 'just nonsense for interviews' and credited the description to Piers Wenger suggesting Moffat needed 'to make a statement about what kind of **Doctor Who** you're going to make.'[143] This seems a touch disingenuous, as the trailer for the season seemed to emphasise the fairytale aspect by deliberately

---

[141] Quoted in Gillat, 'Bigger than **Star Wars**!', p9.

[142] 'Moffat on Matt Smith's Era, Writing the 50th Anniversary and **More**'.

[143] Moffat, **Toby Hadoke's Who's Round** #232.

echoing *Alice in Wonderland* with the Doctor and Amy falling down a hole filled with monsters[144]. The Doctor even explicitly references fairy tales during the episode, specifically pointing out that Amelia's name is 'a bit fairytale'[145]. Whilst not denying that there were often such aspects to the era of the show he oversaw, it is telling that the metaphors he reached for outlined his view of the show as essentially a modern fairytale. In two departure interviews, for the podcast **Toby Hadoke's Who's Round** and the YouTube series **The Fan Show**, he opined that the show is about 'a wizard in a magic box who's got a magic wand,' going so far as to say in the **Fan Show** interview that '**Doctor Who** is like a fairytale because that is the genre it most precisely resembles.'[146] Much as he might deny the description, it is hard to say that there is not a kernel of truth to it, when he describes his view of the show in such terms.[147]

Instead it is far more accurate to say that the element of fairytale is a subset of Moffat's general view of the show. He has consistently

---

[144] A similar presentation to this concluded the tour section of the Doctor Who Experience. It's hard not to believe that it's deliberately designed to appeal to children.

[145] This will later be thrown back at the Doctor when Amelia explains why she is no longer known as Amelia: the rejection of the name as 'a bit fairytale' and therefore a bad thing indicates she has grown up and perhaps lost touch with the wonder of childhood.

[146] 'Steven Moffat on Matt Smith's Era, Writing the 50th Anniversary and **More**'.

[147] Finally, in the penultimate scene of *Twice Upon a Time*, the last **Doctor Who** episode of Moffat's period as showrunner, one Doctor tells another that 'The universe generally fails to be a fairytale, but that's where we come in'.

described **Doctor Who** as a 'children's show'[148], and this is the fundamental difference between his version and Russell T Davies's. Nowhere is this better illustrated than in their respective first episodes. The initial montage of Rose's life in *Rose* frames the show as a contemporary drama: it is deliberately couched in the trappings of modern television. Davies uses characters and settings which would not be out of place in soap operas to draw the audience in before the Doctor disrupts what passes for normality. His main character is employed in a department store rather than still being at school, and Rose is old enough to still be relatable to by children and young people but also by slightly older people in their 20s and 30s. In short, Davies was designing a show to appeal to as wide an age range as possible: on the surface it began by resembling a popular evening drama. With *The Eleventh Hour* Moffat began with a very different approach: although by the episode's end we have a companion of a similar age to Rose, the opening 20 minutes firmly root this version of the show in fairytale and children's literature.

JRR Tolkien defined a fairy story as not depending 'on any definition or historical account of elf or fairy, but upon the nature of **Faërie**: the Perilous Realm itself, and the air that blows there.'[149] In other words, the fairy story is defined by the world entered by the protagonist. The Doctor's universe of monsters and strange worlds is essentially a modern version of the Perilous Realm, cloaked with the science-fiction notion of time travel, and Amelia is the traveller

---

[148] As far back as 1995 (Bishop, David, 'Four Writers, One Discussion') and as late as 2017 (Spilsbury, Tom 'When You Run With the Doctor It Feels Like It Will Never End, But However Hard You Try, You Can't Run Forever', DWM #515, p14).
[149] Tolkien, JRR, *Tolkien on Fairy Stories*, p32.

in that realm. The first shot of Amelia's garden emphasises that we are entering a child's world and takes Tolkien's phrase about the 'air that blows there' literally. The shot is of a child's handheld windmill toy and then a swing buffeted by wind: an obvious metaphor for a safe haven invaded by an unseen force[150] – the land of Faerie comes to Amelia rather than her going to it.

As Frank Collins points out, the direction of this scene 'invests it with mystery, a certain menace and a sense that this is a place where magic is about to happen.'[151] He goes on to note that this echoes tropes of classic children's literature such as *The Secret Garden* (1911) or *Tom's Midnight Garden* (1958). The night-time garden is a blank canvas for the child's imagination, where horror or heroism might lurk: by chance both of these will visit Amelia's garden by the end of the night. In this case her imagination will be proven correct; the mysterious crack in her wall does hide an unimaginable horror, and the mysterious stranger who will visit will lead her to adventures beyond her wildest dreams. Visually, with the saturated darker colours and a relatively brightly dressed heroine, there is an echo of the style of Tim Burton films such as *Sleepy Hollow* (1999), *Charlie and the Chocolate Factory* (2005) or *Alice in Wonderland* (2010)[152]. There are no fairies or monsters at the bottom of this garden:

---

[150] This is a directorial touch: the shooting script (an excerpt from which is reproduced under 'Lesson Plan 1: Introducing the Doctor' at **Doctor Who**: Script to Screen Competition') merely describes a 'fairly big garden. Bit neglected, overgrown, creepy' and specifies only the presence of '...an old, battered garden shed.'

[151] Collins, Frank, *Exploring the Worlds of the Eleventh Doctor*, location 363.

[152] Wright, Mark, ed, *Doctor Who: The Complete History* Volume 63: *The Eleventh Hour, The Beast Below, Victory of the Daleks*, p34.

instead they are in the house in the crack in the wall and an extra invisible room. Amelia's safe haven has been invaded and only the garden is secure as that's where the Doctor lands every time in this story: a reversal of the usual fairy story role where a traveller voyages off a path into the Perilous Realm. With no safe haven from monsters, in this case the safest place for Amelia would be with the wizard on his journeys. She almost has no choice.

This initial scene is notable as it is the first time we have been introduced to a new Doctor through a child's eyes. In the previous stories where a new Doctor has been simultaneously introduced with a new supporting character, our viewpoint characters have been adults: Ian and Barbara in *An Unearthly Child* (1963), Brigadier Lethbridge-Stewart in *Spearhead from Space* (1970), Grace in *Doctor Who* (1996) and Rose in *Rose*. This is a hint that our viewpoint should be a little different: we should perhaps try and look at the world through a child's eyes to get the best from this version of the show. At this point in writing the series Moffat is extremely fond of using a child as a significant character: of his four stories for Russell T Davies three featured significant roles for children (*Blink* being the exception[153]), and Davies even excised a storyline featuring Donna having children in *Turn Left* (2008) saying 'You do better kids!'[154] This use of children in significant roles, relatively unusual in **Doctor Who**, continues in Moffat scripts up to *The Wedding of River Song* (with

---

[153] Even then, the short story which is the source of Blink ('What I did on My Christmas Holidays by Sally Sparrow' from The Doctor Who Annual 2006) features a child protagonist. The change in age may be due to either the practicalities of making an episode with a child as the lead character or the nature of the Weeping Angels meaning this would be inappropriate.

[154] Davies and Cook, *The Writer's Tale*, p302.

the exception of *The Time of Angels / Flesh and Stone* (2010)) but begins to fade somewhat around the time of *Asylum of the Daleks* (2012): his Peter Capaldi scripts in particular see very few significant roles for children, despite the first season partially being set at a school[155].

It is a different strand of children's literature which sets the tone for our initial impression of this Doctor. Instead of a fairytale it is modelled on AA Milne's *The House at Pooh Corner*: specifically, the second chapter, 'In which Tigger comes to the Forest and has breakfast'. It begins with Winnie-the-Pooh being woken up by 'a noise of some kind, made by a strange animal'[156]. After a relatively long exchange of hallos Tigger is invited in (unlike the Doctor he does not depart immediately). Tigger is portrayed as a ball of energy: being described as cheerful, awake early in the morning and wrestling a tablecloth. The remainder of the chapter forms an obvious basis for the 'fish fingers and custard' scene: after declaring the night before that Tiggers 'like everything,'[157] he proceeds to reject the favourite foods of other characters: Pooh's honey, Piglet's haycorns and Eeyore's thistles. On a visit to Kanga's house Pooh only

---

[155] *The Day of the Doctor* appears to be a key point here, with the Doctor's motivations in changing history partially being down to saving Gallifreyan children: this motif of saving children continues through *The Time of the Doctor* and into the Capaldi era with *Listen* and *The Caretaker* (both 2014) and right up to *World Enough and Time / The Doctor Falls*. Children move from characters to an ideal to be cared for: perhaps this change of approach is related to Moffat's own children maturing at this point, or perhaps it is a conscious choice to help distinguish between the two eras.

[156] Milne, AA, *The House at Pooh Corner*, p21.

[157] Milne, *Pooh Corner*, p22.

finds unsuitable foods: 'And he found a small tin of condensed milk, and something seemed to tell him that Tiggers didn't like this.'[158]

Tigger then proceeds to reject everything in the cupboard:

> 'But the more Tigger put his nose into this and his paw into that, the more things he found which Tiggers didn't like. And when he found everything in the cupboard, and couldn't eat any of it he said to Kanga, "What happens now?"'[159]

Finally, when Kanga's child Roo is being fed Extract of Malt as 'strengthening medicine', Tigger takes a 'large galollop' and in a child's food, finally finds something he likes and proceeds to have it 'for breakfast, dinner and tea'[160] and 'sometimes, when Kanga thought he wanted strengthening, he had a spoonful or two of Roo's breakfast after meals as medicine.'[161]

This is a clear model for the 11th Doctor's arrival: Amelia investigating a noise from outside the house and finding a rude stranger, and the following scene with the Doctor rejecting conventional foods ('Beans are evil – bad bad beans'), before arriving at fish fingers and custard – a child's idea of a meal, with two favourites mixed together regardless of suitability. He may not eat the dish for 'breakfast, dinner and tea' but he clearly remains fond of it, even if only for its association with Amelia: in *The Time of the Doctor* when Clara discovers him in the TARDIS immediately prior to

---

[158] Milne, *Pooh Corner*, p34.
[159] Milne, *Pooh Corner*, p36.
[160] Milne, *Pooh Corner*, p37.
[161] Milne, *Pooh Corner*, p37.

his regeneration she finds a half eaten bowl of fish fingers and custard[162].

More pertinently this sets the tone for this incarnation – it's hard not to think that this portrayal of Tigger is a model for Smith's performance: like Tigger he is friendly but endearingly rude in a childish manner – rather than asking, he demands 'you're Scottish – fry something!'[163] Despite being newly regenerated, he is easily as energetic as Tigger: he pops his head from the TARDIS like a jack-in-the-box and paces up and down while Amelia tries to find him food.

The strange forces in Amelia's house, including the crack in the wall, are not specifically drawn from fairytales or children's literature but rather from Moffat's personal experience. The notion of the 'crack in time' was based on an actual crack in one of the bedrooms in Moffat's house:

> 'There was a crack along the wall above my younger son Louis' bed. There was a roughly smile-shaped crack, which I didn't point out to him because I thought he may never sleep again.'[164]

This is the imagination of a father and a storyteller: imagining what a child may think about a crack in his wall. The other strange element

---

[162] 'Fish fingers and custard' also appears to be a literary reference, to a 1982 **Listen with Mother** story by Jane Holiday: it subsequently appeared on Noel Edmonds' radio show and on vinyl record read by Clement Freud (Castle, Paul, 'An Old Recipe?', DWM #517, p10).

[163] That Amelia is able to safely use a cooker marks her out as having an independent streak, even at such an early age.

[164] **Doctor Who Confidential:** *Call Me the Doctor.*

of Amy's house, the extra room, was taken from Moffat's own childhood. It was:

> 'inspired by Moffat recalling visits to his grandmother's house in Wolverhampton during his childhood and having a recurring dream of a non-existant [sic] extra room in her house.'[165]

Again, without being a specific reference, it is drawn from the dreams of a child with all the attendant importance and connotations of a dream.

While the sequences with the grown-up Amy may not be specifically fairytale in presentation they can be seen to be possible references: the coma patients are in thrall to Prisoner Zero, locked in an enchanted sleep in the manner of Snow White or Sleeping Beauty; part of the Doctor's triumph is to wake Amy (the princess who needs rescuing) from her enchanted sleep, and thereby a monstrous influence, late in the episode. Prisoner Zero itself is serpentine in nature and shape-changing, a potential reference to the serpent in the Garden of Eden, although here it is the Doctor who tempts Amy with the apple, the symbol of forbidden knowledge: a warning that perhaps he is not entirely as pure of intention as he appears to be[166]. He is, however, the man who makes it 'safe to be scared again';[167] who guards us from monsters. This is an important element of the modern fairytale:

---

[165] Wright, *The Complete History* Volume 63, p23.
[166] As demonstrated by his not informing Amy that he is taking her on board partly due to a mystery he needs to solve, and later in the season when he conceals Rory's (first) death from her.
[167] *The Curse of Fatal Death.*

'Fairytales are more than true: not because they tell us that dragons exist, but because they tell us that dragons can be beaten.'[168]

In Steven Moffat's conception of the show the Doctor is the one who makes the world safe for us and chases the monsters away: he metaphorically slays the dragon Amy ends up in thrall to by having Prisoner Zero recaptured, and then underlines this by banishing the Atraxi, thereby preserving the Earth from threat now and in the future. This last scene emphasises that this is and has always been the Doctor's role, first by playing a series of threats he has faced and then by showing the Doctor's previous faces[169]. The effect of this is immediately to embed this version of **Doctor Who** as the same show we have seen before: it is perfectly logical that **Doctor Who** is, was, and always has been a modern fairytale.

---

[168] Gaiman, Neil, *Coraline*, p2. Although this epigraph is attributed to GK Chesterton it is actually a paraphrase.
[169] Although he is still evidently blanking out the horrors of his time as the War Doctor at this point.

CHAPTER 5: 'SILENCE WILL FALL'

Although Russell T Davies had introduced the arc storyline as a regular feature of the series[170], this tended to consist of little more than a series of clues dropped in throughout the season. Broadly speaking, the arc in his first two seasons essentially consisted of a mysterious recurring phrase, the third a series of clues relating to the Master and his disguises as Professor Yana and Harold Saxon, and the fourth a mention of disappearing planets[171]. In line with series such as **Buffy the Vampire Slayer** (1997-2003), they had a minimal impact on the story of the week (or fortnight), and seemed designed so that even a casual viewer who didn't watch every episode might be able to pick up on them. With Davies in charge the emphasis was on an emotional arc, playing the Doctor and companion's relationship out across an entire season. Essentially, aside from the third series, the story is the empowerment of a companion: represented literally with Rose becoming the Bad Wolf and Donna becoming the Doctor-Donna, with all of the Doctor's knowledge. In Martha's case her actions in the year between *The Sound of Drums* and *Last of the Time Lords* (both 2007) in particular give her the

---

[170] The first explicit arc story is the show's 16th season (1978-79), which revolved around the search for the Key to Time, although it can be argued that the Doctor's attempts to return Ian and Barbara home constituted an earlier rudimentary arc. Whether the show's 23rd season (1986) counts as an arc story is debatable: although produced in three blocks and novelised in four it was broadcast as one 14-part story.

[171] Rose has a series of inessential cameos during the season; however, these do not have a substantial narrative impact until *Turn Left*, the episode preceding the season finale.

strength to leave the Doctor as she realizes she doesn't need him anymore.

The Eleventh Hour begins a different approach, one more reliant on an underlying plot and which looks to play out storylines over longer than a season. Moffat's initial idea was for Matt Smith's Doctor to be involved in some kind of war at the end of his life, with 'pre-shocks' of this happening throughout his lifetime up 'like a persistent friend': this would have ended with the Doctor chained to a cliff[172]. Although this was the overall plan, and one which is reasonably close to what would eventually happen, the image which inspired the ending is notably absent[173]. While the story of Prisoner Zero and the Atraxi is the main story, and is resolved within the episode's running time, the episode itself introduces three more separate but related stories running which will be resolved over varying timeframes, two of which will recur at significant points in the 11th Doctor's story.

The first is the 'crack in the wall', introduced in the Amelia's childhood section of the story; the second and third are introduced in the final showdown between the Doctor and Prisoner Zero (the Pandorica and 'silence will fall'); and lastly there is the ongoing story of Amy and Rory's wedding, whose resolution will be bound up with the story of the crack in time. Unlike the approach of Russell T

---

[172] Moffat, Steven, onstage at Gallifrey One convention, February 2018.

[173] It can, however, be argued that the Doctor is metaphorically chained to the village of Christmas on Trenzalore by his own values and morality.

Davies[174], these will impact on the narrative at several significant points. The crack in the wall remains an unsolved mystery at the end of *The Eleventh Hour*. Within the fiction of the series this is the day after the Amy finally gets to join the Doctor on his adventures, and the date of her wedding[175]. It is a signifier that the questions surrounding Amy's marriage and the cracks in time are a time-limited mystery which will essentially be resolved by the end of the season. The difference between this and Davies's arcs is that as well as being a visual motif which will recur through several stories[176], it will narratively impact individual stories within the season: the crack becomes important in resolving the plot of *The Time of Angels / Flesh and Stone*, at first creating a threat to Amy and the clerics and then being essential to defeating the Weeping Angels. *Flesh and Stone* also features an appearance by a Doctor from the future, something that will not be explained until the finale. The crack also reappears at the climax to *The Hungry Earth / Cold Blood*, in which it 'eats' Rory's dead body and the Doctor also finds a fragment of the TARDIS inside[177]. These are points which will prove important to the plot of

---

[174] With the arguable exception of the Chameleon Arch whose use in *Human Nature / The Family of Blood* (2007) foreshadowed the key plot twist in *Utopia* (2007).

[175] In, the real world, the date of the broadcast of *The Big Bang*. As discussed in Chapter 3 of Purser-Hallard, Philip, *The Black Archive #4: Dark Water / Death in Heaven*, this is not the only example of Moffat using broadcast dates within the fiction to give the episode an extra resonance.

[176] *The Beast Below* and *Victory of the Daleks* (2010).

[177] *Victory of the Daleks* and Russell T Davies's novelisation of *Rose* show the cracks spreading forwards as well as backwards in time. Their appearance in the latter are a clue to how time works in **Doctor Who**: the cracks do not revise history until they have happened, but

The Pandorica Opens / The Big Bang (2010): in particular, it renders *The Time of Angels / Flesh and Stone* indivisible from the overall story and unable to function without it in a way which does not occur in the Davies era[178]. However, while the story of the cracks in time is resolved in *The Big Bang* it deliberately leaves open the question of what 'silence' falling means: prior to the attempt to destroy the TARDIS we see the words on the TARDIS scanner with still no clue as to what they may mean.

What is perhaps more interesting in terms of the show's narrative structure is the setting up of the Silence arc story. This is done very briefly in *The Eleventh Hour*, as Prisoner Zero's final taunt to the Doctor before the Atraxi recapture him: 'The universe is cracked. The Pandorica will open and silence will fall.'

This would initially seem to indicate that the 'silence will fall' arc is indivisibly related to the Pandorica, which is revealed in *The Pandorica Opens* as the intended ultimate trap for the Doctor. However, the nature of the 'silence will fall' prophecy seems to preclude this[179]. This reference actually seeds the arc we will see

---

once their effect has spread the changes it wreaks have always happened. 'Timey wimey' may well be a plot device to save the sanity of fans while simultaneously undermining the notion of a definitive canon. (Davies, Russell T., *Rose*, p83)

[178] Although *The Long Game* sets up the world seen in *Bad Wolf / The Parting of the Ways* (all 2005), it functions as a standalone story.

[179] 'Silence will fall when the oldest question is answered.' This question is eventually revealed to be the one implicit in the title of the series: 'Doctor who?' If the Doctor was trapped for eternity in the Pandorica he would never be able to answer this question, silence wouldn't fall and the Time Lords would not return. Perhaps the Alliance seen in *The Pandorica Opens* actually want the Time

played out in the second series and even, eventually, the events which culminate in the 11th Doctor's regeneration. It is called back to in *The Vampires of Venice* (2010), explicitly linking the Silence and the cracks in time:

ROSANNA

We ran from the Silence. Why are you here?

DOCTOR

Wedding present. The Silence?

ROSANNA

There were cracks. Some were tiny. Some were as big as the sky. Through some we saw worlds and people, and through others we saw Silence and the end of all things.

This is notable as, although it appears to be a simple reminder of the cracks in time, it also foreshadows the appearance of the Silence, without providing details. The usage of the phrase in *The Eleventh Hour* and *Vampires in Venice* seems to indicate an event of some kind. It is eventually revealed to be part of a prophecy which will only gradually unravel at the end of Smith's tenure: the species known as the Silence have adopted the name in reference to this prophecy. The changing nature of the phrase 'silence', between the prophecy and the species may indicate either a verbal sleight of hand on Moffat's part or, alternatively, a change of plan: or as seen with **Babylon 5 (1993-98)** and **Lost** (2004-10), while there may be an overall plan it may alternatively be a simple creative reaction to a

---

Lords to return? Or perhaps the events of *The Day of the Doctor* mean history has changed and so has the nature of the prophecy.

good idea coming along and being incorporated. The essence of the plan may have altered, but the demands of making 14 episodes of **Doctor Who** a year mean the details will likely remain in flux until the last minute.

As Moffat put it on stage at Gallifrey One: 'you never know how things are going to work out [...] you've got to have 28 different exits.' This need for differing plans would become a major issue in series 6, with Moffat writing himself into a corner. The Silence arc involved the kidnapping of a pregnant Amy and then her child. Moffat felt that this would trivialise a serious issue in the service of entertainment, and that he could not use what would be a serious issue in a show which could not support this:

> 'You can't portray that fantastical, whimsical sci-fi bereavement as the real thing, when the real thing has been endured by people in the audience. You'd be trivialising real-life tragedy. So I just cut forward several months and rather ducked the issue. They processed that not-quite-loss offscreen, which I wasn't crazy about.'[180]

This led to the arc having a rather broken feel in the middle: the end of *A Good Man Goes to War* (2011) feels like the beginning of a significant strand of story but *Let's Kill Hitler* (2011) flagrantly does not follow up on this promise, and essentially sees the season storyline being parked for several episodes. It also has the unfortunate effect of making Rory and Amy seem blackly callous in *Night Terrors* (2011) when Rory makes fun of the idea of searching

---

[180] Quoted in Cook, Benjamin, 'When I agreed to do one more run, I thought "Sod It, I'm Not Doing The March to the Scaffold. I Want It To Feel Like a Brand New Show"', DWM #502, p20.

for a lost child. Where the arc of series 5 functions coherently, following the first half of the season the arc of series 6 is something of a mess, culminating in a second consecutive series finale set on an alternative Earth.

Moffat would ultimately resolve the motivations of the Silence in *The Time of the Doctor*, and also manage to tie this into the events of the arc initiated by the first appearance of an iteration of Clara Oswald in *Asylum of the Daleks*, and into *The Day of the Doctor*. While this can perhaps occasionally seem clumsy[181], it can also be regarded as elegant in places: where better to (perhaps) bury the Doctor than a place he defended for several human lifetimes? Inevitably attempting to produce a long-form arc for television will be riddled with compromises, but the attempted plotting of a Doctor's era as one long-form story should be admired as one of **Doctor Who**'s grand follies: a Quixote like tilting at a windmill. In that respect *The Eleventh Hour* marks the beginning of the most grandly ambitious era in the show's history.

---

[181] For instance, why do the cracks in time reappear when they should have been healed in *The Big Bang*? And the Doctor visits the once-feared Trenzalore twice in three stories – perhaps the state of the planet in *The Name of the Doctor* (2013) shows that even his centuries-long stand is futile.

CONCLUSION: 'ALL OF TIME AND SPACE'

'I'm more interested in beginnings.'

(Steven Moffat)[182]

Steven Moffat's time as showrunner ended two minutes before the end of *Twice Upon a Time* (2017), with an injunction to laugh hard, run fast and be kind. His era ends with the last word of his last script being exactly the same last word as that of Russell T Davies's last script[183]. In many ways it could be regarded as an archetypal Steven Moffat script: it features multiple time zones, technology gone wrong rather than an outright villain, an artificial afterlife, multiple kisses to the show's past, an excuse to crowbar in an appearance by a Dalek, and, with Capaldi's last speech, the notion that **Doctor Who** is essentially for children ('children can hear your name...'). It's an elegant summing up of what might be seen as Moffat's major themes, and rounds off his era appropriately. Where he started with the youngest Doctor meeting a child, he ends with the oldest actor to play the Doctor as an ongoing part meeting his oldest self: the shock of the new giving way to age and reflection. It's a long way from *The Eleventh Hour*.

The Eleventh Hour is essentially an episode of promise in every sense: a fresh era with a new Doctor and new companion, a new approach and the promise that every new era needs to make – that the show will be as exciting as it has always been. In that respect *The Eleventh Hour* remains a remarkable success: DWM's 50th

---

[182] Onstage at Gallifrey One convention, February 2018.
[183] It's 'go': it could be read as self-instruction or an instruction to his successor.

anniversary poll saw it as the 17th best story in **Doctor Who**'s history[184], and in the year after it was broadcast the show became the BBC's biggest selling show internationally[185]. For a show which even its showrunner had doubts would last, it was a remarkable success. Its legacy is that its success secured the show's future by proving that an old show could be exciting all over again in new clothes: when Chris Chibnall succeeded Moffat he had no such insecurity, with a Memorandum of Understanding signed with Shanghai Media Group suggesting that the BBC intended making at least five more series[186].

The proof that the show did not depend on the presence of either David Tennant or Russell T Davies, but could be successful with new lead actors and writers, essentially gives it not only security but the freedom to make creatively bold decisions, such as casting an older lead and then its first female lead. It provided its leads with successful careers: Matt Smith starred in prestige Netflix drama **The Crown** (2016-), and Karen Gillan is easily the most successful former **Doctor Who** companion, adding a part in the 2017 remake of *Jumanji* to a recurring role in the **Marvel** cinematic universe since *Guardians of the Galaxy* (2014). No other companion has a remotely similar film career.

---

[184] Three of the episodes which bested it were also Steven Moffat scripts.

[185] Sweeney, Mark, 'Doctor Who BBC Worldwide's Biggest-Selling TV Show Internationally'.

[186] 'The deal not only covers showrunners Russell T Davies and Steven Moffat's series 1-10, but also incoming showrunner Chris Chibnall's yet-to-film series 11, as well as a first look for series 12-15' ('**Doctor Who** Gets Brand Boost in China').

Simultaneously it also established Steven Moffat as the most successful British television writer of the decade: on top of showrunning **Doctor Who** he would co-run **Sherlock**, a wildly successful transplant of Sherlock Holmes into the 21st century of computers and mobile phones. In short, in its way, it was as successful as *Rose* had been at re-establishing the series five years earlier. It ended with an offer to Amy (and by extension the audience) of all of time and all space, proving that there is little as exciting as a new beginning – something **Doctor Who** is almost uniquely placed to offer on a regular basis. Everything that was old was new again; just as it would be eight years later.

APPENDIX – TARDIS CUTAWAY

The Blu-ray release of the fifth series in late 2010 was accompanied by an extra scene which bridged the small narrative gap between *The Eleventh Hour* and *The Beast Below* (2010)[187], effectively marking them out as two halves of a story in the same way *Rose* and *The End of the World* (2005) were[188]. While the narrative of the series as transmitted does not suffer if these scenes are omitted, they add texture with interesting details.

The main thrust of the mini-episode is Amy's reaction to entering the Doctor's world: the sense of wonder we see at the end of *The Eleventh Hour* doesn't last five minutes. Instead, once the shock of the new has worn off she begins asking questions that have rarely been asked: why a police box; how does the air stay in if the outside is made of wood[189]; and if there's a light on top does he need to change the bulb? This is a continuation of Moffat's habit of picking at picking at questions which may have vexed fans over the years: one that begun with his short story 'Continuity Errors', which questioned the why the Doctor does things the way he does when time travel gives him the power to remake the universe as he chooses[190], and continued through his exploration of the Doctor's

---

[187] Much as the **Children in Need** scene in 2005 had done for the Eccleston-Tennant regeneration.

[188] Although they do not link narratively, they do thematically: *Rose* and *The Eleventh Hour* see the Doctor enter the companion's world, *The End of the World* and *The Beast Below* see the companion entering the Doctor's world.

[189] Although the rational answer is that it isn't wood, the cutting off of the air supply in *Planet of the Daleks* suggests there's no easy answer to this.

[190] This might be termed a god complex.

attitude to sexuality in *The Empty Child / The Doctor Dances* and *The Girl in the Fireplace*[191]. With this kind of fannish concern and puncturing of the atmosphere of wonder, it is easy to see why it was bequeathed to the fan audience rather than the general viewer: the impact of both the ending of *The Eleventh Hour* and the beginning of *The Beast Below* as transmitted depend to an extent on retaining Amy's sense of wonder. Her queries here and Moffat's trademark flippant answers to these questions rather undermine that[192].

This scene also underlines that Amy is aware of the conventions of the science fiction genre[193], much as Rose was in *The Empty Child / The Doctor Dances* ('Gimme some Spock!')[194]. Her questions indicate different expectations of advanced technology: why would a time machine be made of wood and look like an Earth object she is unfamiliar with? She also asks the Doctor if he is alien; whether his human appearance is simply a disguise; whether he is 'a space squid'

---

[191] This kind of concern with the show's own myths will recur throughout Moffat's tenure, most prominently with the arc regarding the Doctor's name which underpins the stories featuring the Silence and even extends to Peter Capaldi's final monologue in *Twice Upon a Time*.

[192] Moffat's approach rather underlines that there are no real definitive answers to many such fandom debates and that any supposedly definitive answer may be rendered redundant by stories told by future production crews.

[193] The Doctor is perhaps also aware of genre tropes: his joke about an interdimensional alien being affected by wood may be a reference to the golden age Green Lantern, whose ring of power could not affect wood.

[194] This comment is mildly out of character for Rose, who displays little affection for or awareness of science fiction outside this.

or '...a tiny little slug in a human suit'[195]. While we have never seen a Gallifreyan regenerate into a non-humanoid form[196], equally the disregard of the regenerative process for ethnicity or gender suggests that a more alien form is a possibility: what's to stop a Time Lord taking the form of a Silurian, an Ogri or even a Dalek for example? As with 'Continuity Errors', Moffat is questioning the show's fundamental precepts with jokes.

The final important element of this short scene is the ending, which leads directly into the scene following the opening credits of *The Beast Below*. While we see the Doctor there dangling Amy out of the TARDIS[197], we do not see the events that lead them there until this scene, with the Doctor pushing Amy out of the doors. This action suggests that perhaps it is best not to trust the Doctor blindly, and also that he has an incredible degree of faith in the reliability of the TARDIS[198]. The effect is to derail Amy's querying of his nature and

---

[195] This may be a reference to the Ceti eels seen in **Star Trek**: *The Wrath of Khan*, Brain Slugs of **Futurama** or possibly the alien life forms seen in the film *Slither* (2005), where a parasitic sluglike organism turns humans into squidlike monsters. Or, most plausibly, an in-joke referencing the character of the Collector in *The Sun Makers* (1977).

[196] The Master's appearance as a slime in *Doctor Who (1996)* is clearly not the result of a regeneration.

[197] Moffat's era as showrunner is fond of having characters dangle from the TARDIS: the Doctor in both *The Eleventh Hour* and *The Day of the Doctor*, Brian Williams in *Dinosaurs on a Spaceship* (2012) and Clara in *Face the Raven* (2015). Chris Chibnall is potentially spoofing this when the 13th Doctor hangs out of the door, then falls out, in *Twice Upon a Time*.

[198] Though as we see in *The Time of Angels / Flesh and Stone*, this confidence is not misplaced.

engage her with a degree of wonder once more – this Doctor does not seem to want to reveal too much of his identity even to those who are ostensibly closest to him. This is a characteristic which will play out across the 11th Doctor's era, and arguably end up being his fundamental character flaw. The great question of the Matt Smith era is the meaning of 'who' in 'Doctor Who', and it is only when he faces up to this question, his own identity and who he is that he eventually truly finds his purpose: standing up and taking responsibility for defending the village of Christmas for lifetimes rather than simply wandering the universe, dodging responsibility and looking for adventures. In that sense, this Doctor will have the same kind of fulfilling ending as the War Doctor and his ninth self.

BIBLIOGRAPHY

Books

Alderman, Naomi, *Borrowed Time*. **Doctor Who**. London, BBC Books, 2011. ISBN 9781849902335.

Arnold, Jon, *Rose*. **The Black Archive** #1. Edinburgh, Obverse Books, 2016. ISBN 9781909031371.

Burk, Graeme, and Robert Smith?, *Who is the Doctor*. Toronto, ECW Press, 2012. ISBN 9781550229844.

Cartmel, Andrew, *Cat's Cradle: Warhead*. **Doctor Who: The New Adventures**. London, Virgin Publishing Ltd, 1992. ISBN 9780426203674.

Cartmel, Andrew, *Warlock*. **Doctor Who: The New Adventures**, London, Virgin Publishing Ltd, 1995. ISBN 978042626204336.

Cartmel, Andrew, *Warchild*. **Doctor Who: The New Adventures**, London, Virgin Publishing Ltd, 1996. ISBN 9780426204640.

Colgan, Jenny T, *The Christmas Invasion*. **Doctor Who: Target Collection**. London, BBC Books, 2018. ISBN 9781785943287.

Collins, Frank, *The Pandorica Opens: Exploring the Worlds of the 11th Doctor*. Cambridge, Classic TV Press, 2010. ISBN 9780956100023.

Cook, Benjamin, *Doctor Who: The New Audio Adventures – The Inside Story*. Maidenhead, Big Finish Productions, 2003. ISBN 9781844350347.

Cornell, Paul, ed, *Professor Bernice Summerfield and the Dead Men Diaries*. London, Big Finish Productions, 1999, ISBN 9781903654002.

Davies, Russell T, *Rose*. **Doctor Who: Target Collection**. London, BBC Books, 2018. ISBN 9781785943263.

Davies, Russell T, and Benjamin Cook, *The Writer's Tale: The Final Chapter*. London, BBC Books, 2010. ISBN 9781846078613.

Davison, Peter, *Is There Life Outside the Box?: An Actor Despairs*. London, John Blake Publishing Ltd, 2016. ISBN 9781786061126.

Hickman, Clayton, ed, *The Doctor Who Annual 2006*. Tunbridge Wells, Panini, 2005. ISBN 9781904419730.

Moffat, Steven, 'What I did on My Christmas Holidays by Sally Sparrow'.

Gaiman, Neil, *Coraline*. London, Bloomsbury Publishing, 2002. ISBN 9781408808191.

Howe, David J, Mark Stammers and Stephen James Walker, *Doctor Who: The Television Companion*. London, BBC Books, 1998. ISBN 9780563405887.

James, Clive, *Play All: A Bingewatcher's Notebook*. Padstow, Yale University Press, 201., ISBN 9780300218091.

Lane, Andy, and Justin Richards, eds, *Decalog 3: Consequences*. **Doctor Who**. London, Virgin Publishing. 1996, ISBN 9780426204787.

Moffat, Steven, 'Continuity Errors'.

Milne, AA, *The House at Pooh Corner*. London, Methuen & Co Ltd, 1928. Facsimile edition 2011. ISBN 9781405255820.

Moffat, Steven, *The Day of the Doctor*. **Doctor Who: Target Collection**. London, BBC Books, 2018. ISBN 9781785943294.

Parkin, Lance, *The Doctor Who Fanzine Archives* Vol 1: Lance Parkin.

Time Unincorporated #1. Des Moines, Mad Norwegian Press, 2009. ISBN 9781935234012.

Purser-Hallard, Philip, *Dark Water / Death in Heaven*. **The Black Archive** #4. Edinburgh, Obverse Books, 2016. ISBN 9781909031401.

Tolkien, JRR, *Tolkien on Fairy Stories*. London, HarperCollins, 2014. ISBN 9780007582914.

Periodicals

Breakfast at Czar's.

> O'Brien, Steve, 'Picking Up the Pieces'. *Breakfast at Czar's* #1, January 1994.

> O'Brien, Steve, '*Dead Line*: Dead?'. *Breakfast at Czar's* #1, January 1994.

Doctor Who: The Complete History. Volume 63: *The Eleventh Hour, The Beast Below, Victory of the Daleks*, 9 August 2017.

Doctor Who Magazine (DWM). Marvel UK, Panini, BBC, 1979-.

> Castle, Paul, An Old Recipe?. DWM #517, cover date November 2017.

> Cook, Benjamin, 'This Is It. I'm Going to Push the Button. When I Do There's No Going Back. I'm About to End What Will Be the Best Job I Ever Have'. DWM #500, cover date July 2016.

> Cook, Benjamin, 'When I Agreed To Do One More Run, I Thought "Sod It, I'm Not Doing the March to the Scaffold. I Want It To Feel Like a Brand New Show"'. DWM #502, cover date September 2016.

> Cook, Benjamin, 'The Last Battle'. DWM #521, cover date

February 2018.

Gillat, Gary, 'We're Gonna Be Bigger than **Star Wars**!' DWM #279, cover date June 1999.

Moffat, Steven, 'Ask Steven Moffat', DWM #459, cover date May 2013.

Pixley, Andrew, 'Just Like Starting Over', *The Doctor Who Companion: Series 5 Volume 1*, cover date August 2010.

Spilsbury, Tom, 'The Time is Now!'. DWM #418, cover date March 2010.

Spilsbury, Tom, 'When You Run With the Doctor, It Feels Like It Will Never End, But However Hard You Try, You Can't Run Forever'. DWM #515, cover date September 2017.

Mulkern, Patrick and Mark Braxton, *Radio Times: Doctor Who – The Companions*, November 2010.

Television

Alan Carr: Chatty Man. Open Mike Productions, 2009-.

Babylon 5. Babylonian Productions Ltd, Synthetic Worlds Ltd, 1993-98.

Buffy the Vampire Slayer. Mutant Enemy Productions, 1997-2003.

Casanova. Red Production Company, Powercorp, BBC Films, 2005.

Chalk. Pola Jones, 1997.

Coupling. Hartswood Films, 2000-04.

Doctor Who. BBC, 1963-.

Doctor Who Confidential. BBC, 2005-11.

>   *Call Me the Doctor*, 2010.

Joking Apart. BBC, 1991-95.

Lost. Bad Robot, Touchstone Television, ABC Studios, 2004-10.

Press Gang. Richmond Film and Television, 1989-93.

>   *How to Make a Killing*, 1989.
>
>   *Monday - Tuesday*, 1989.
>
>   *Breakfast at Czar's*, 1990.
>
>   *Something Terrible*, 1990.
>
>   *Day Dreams*, 1992.
>
>   *UnXpected*, 1992.
>
>   *There Are Crocodiles*, 1993.

Sherlock. Hartswood Films, BBC, 2010-.

>   *A Scandal in Belgravia*, 2012.
>
>   *The Abominable Bride*, 2016.
>
>   *The Final Problem*, 2017.

Film

Morahan, Christopher, dir, *Clockwise*, Thorn EMI Screen Entertainment, Moment Films, 1986.

Phillips, Tod, *The Hangover*, Warner Bros, Legendary Entertainment, Green Hat Films, 2009.

Radio

Desert Island Discs, BBC, 1942-.

> *Matt Smith*, 4 March 2018.

Web

'**Doctor Who**: Script to Screen Competition'. BBC Schools. http://www.bbc.co.uk/schools/teachers/doctorwhocompetition/resources.shtml. Accessed 8 April 2018.

'**Doctor Who** Gets Brand Boost in China'. BBC Worldwide, 25 May 2017. http://www.bbc.co.uk/mediacentre/worldwide/2017/doctor-who-china. Accessed 29 March 2018.

'**Doctor Who**'s Steven Moffat – "Matt Smith is like a young man built by old men from memory"'. *The Guardian*, 29 August 2010. https://www.theguardian.com/media/video/2010/aug/29/doctor-who-casting-video. Accessed 29 March 2018.

'New **Doctor Who** Series Confirmed'. BBC News, 30 March 2005. http://news.bbc.co.uk/1/hi/entertainment/4395147.stm. Accessed 30 March 2018.

'Steven Moffat on Matt Smith's Era, Writing the 50th Anniversary and **More**'. **Doctor Who: The Fan Show**. YouTube, 17 January 2018. https://www.youtube.com/watch?v=ZOfIIqb8Uhg. Accessed 30 March 2018.

'TV Since 1981'. BARB. http://www.barb.co.uk/resources/tv-facts/tv-since-1981/2005/top10/. Accessed 30 March 2018.

Bishop, David, 'Four Writers, One Discussion'. New Zealand Doctor

Who Fan Club.
http://doctorwho.org.nz/archive/tsv43/onediscussion.html.
Accessed 29 March 2018.

Dowell, Ben, 'Was Chiwetel Ejiofor the black actor offered the role
of the 11th Doctor ahead of Matt Smith?'. *Radio Times*, 3 June
2016. http://www.radiotimes.com/news/2016-06-03/was-
chiwetel-ejiofor-the-black-actor-offered-the-role-of-the-11th-
doctor-ahead-of-matt-smith/. Accessed 29 March 2018.

Hadoke, Toby, 'Episode #232: Steven Moffat'. **Toby Hadoke's
Who's Round**. https://www.bigfinish.com/ranges/released/toby-
hadoke-s-who-s-round. Accessed 29 March 2018.

Hale, Mike, 'A Brand-New Time Lord, but He Sounds Familiar'. *New
York Times*, 16 April 2010.
https://www.nytimes.com/2010/04/17/arts/television/17who.htm
Accessed 15 April 2018.

Jones, Jane Clare, 'Is Sherlock Sexist? Steven Moffat's Wanton
Women'. *The Guardian*, 3 January 2012.
https://www.theguardian.com/commentisfree/2012/jan/03/sherlo
ck-sexist-steven-moffat. Accessed 29 March 2018.

Leslie, Ian, 'Watch It While It Lasts: Our Golden Age of Television'.
Financial Times, 13 April 2017.
https://www.ft.com/content/68309b3a-1f02-11e7-a454-
ab04428977f9. Accessed 29 March 2018

Martin, Daniel, 'Doctor Who: Matt Smith's Debut in the Eleventh
Hour – the verdict'. *The Guardian*, 3 April 2010.
https://www.theguardian.com/tv-and-
radio/tvandradioblog/2010/apr/03/doctor-who-eleventh-hour.

Accessed 15 April 2018.

Romana, Aja, 'Why does the man behind **Doctor Who** and **Sherlock** still have a job?' *The Daily Dot*, 11 December 2015. https://www.dailydot.com/via/steven-moffat-sexism-sherlock-doctor-who/. Accessed 29 March 2018.

Shulz, Kyle Robert, 'The Overexposure of Clara Oswald'. *Doctor Who* TV, 18 December 2015.http://www.doctorwhotv.co.uk/the-overexposure-of-clara-oswald-79007.htm. Accessed 29 March 2018.

Stavri, Zoe, 'Irene Adler: How to Butcher a Brilliant Woman Character'. Another Angry Woman, 1 January 2012. https://anotherangrywoman.com/2012/01/01/irene-adler-how-to-butcher-a-brilliant-woman-character/. Accessed 29 March 2018.

Sweeney, Mark, 'Doctor Who BBC Worldwide's Biggest-Selling TV Show Internationally'. *The Guardian*, 12 July 2011. https://www.theguardian.com/media/2011/jul/12/doctor-who-bbc-worldwide. Accessed 29 March 2018.

Torsten, 'Alan Watkins, the Young Fogey, and Dressing Like an Englishman'. https://sartorialnotes.com/2016/09/14/alan-watkins-the-young-fogey-and-dressing-like-an-englishman/. Accessed 15 April 2018.

BIOGRAPHY

Jon Arnold is the author of *The Black Archive #1: Rose* and *The Black Archive #10: Scream of the Shalka*, and the co-editor of *Shooty Dog Thing: 2th and Claw* and *Me and the Starman*. He has contributed to 11 essay collections including *Hating to Love* and *Outside In*, and to innumerable fanzines and websites such as *The Two Unfortunates* and *We Are Cult*.

His fiction has appeared in *Shelf Life, Seasons of War, Terrors of the Theatre Diabolique, Secret Invasion: Tales of Eldritch Horrors from the West Country, A Second Target for Tommy* and *A Time Lord for Change.* He is currently writing a Silver Archive on **Buffy the Vampire Slayer**.

He lives in Belfast with his wife and son.

Coming Soon